100
GREATS

HULL
RUGBY LEAGUE FOOTBALL CLUB

100
GREATS

HULL
RUGBY LEAGUE FOOTBALL CLUB

WRITTEN BY
RAYMOND FLETCHER

TEMPUS

First published 2002
Copyright © Raymond Fletcher, 2002

Tempus Publishing Limited
The Mill, Brimscombe Port,
Stroud, Gloucestershire, GL5 2QG

ISBN 0 7524 2429 7

Typesetting and origination by
Tempus Publishing Limited
Printed in Great Britain by
Midway Colour Print, Wiltshire

Hull's 1958 Championship-winning team line up before beating Workington Town in the final at Odsal Stadium, Bradford. From left to right, back row (100 Greats players in capitals): CYRIL SYKES, Alan Holdstock, Brian Saville, Peter Whiteley, Geoff Dannatt, PETER BATESON, MICK SCOTT. Front row: Brian Cooper, Brian Hambling, TOMMY FINN, JOHNNY WHITELEY, IVOR WATTS, Frank Broadhurst.

INTRODUCTION

Hull have not had 100 great players. That was the expected reaction of some when told I was writing a book entitled *100 Hull Greats*. They could be right if the players were to be judged on their standing in rugby league's world rankings: after all, only thirty-seven Hull players have appeared for Great Britain while at The Boulevard. However, in the context of the club's history, I have no doubt that each of the 100 players in this book deserves to be regarded as a great Hull player. In fact, it has pained me to leave out a few others, over whom I agonised before omitting.

Before compiling the century list, I decided on some qualification rules. The two major ones were that it would include every player who represented Great Britain as a Hull player and all those who have made more than 275 appearances for the Airlie Birds. Playing in a Test match is regarded as the pinnacle of a player's achievement, although I have to admit that it has meant the inclusion of one or two players that would not otherwise have been selected. Also, anyone who has played 275 or more times for Hull must surely deserve a place among the club's elite.

I have also introduced a minimum qualification of 30 appearances, which a player must have made for Hull before being considered for entry. This eliminates some top Australian players who were no doubt outstanding but did not stay long enough to be regarded as *Hull Greats*. Unfortunately, this means Jason Smith did not quite qualify before the 2002 deadline, although I have little doubt that another season will confirm the Australian as one of Hull's best ever signings.

Also not taken into consideration is the form and record of players before Hull and twenty-one other clubs broke away from the English Rugby Union in 1895 to form the Northern Union, the forerunner of the Rugby Football League. This is a book about great Hull rugby league players.

Even with the qualification rules being adhered to, it still left over forty places to be filled with my own personal choices, and this is certainly where the arguments will begin. Not so much, I think, with the players selected but with some that are left out. But then most of us will agree that every player who has donned the famous black and white jersey was great for at least a day.

Raymond Fletcher,
February 2002

Front cover: Two Great Britain members of the present Hull FC squad who are included in the club's *100 Greats*. The experienced Lee Jackson, who made 11 Test appearances as a Hull player, is backed up by young international newcomer Paul King.

Back cover: A trio of truly great players who dominated three wonderful eras for Hull FC (from top to bottom): Steve Norton (1978-87), Johnny Whiteley (1950-65) and Billy Batten (1913-23).

ACKNOWLEDGEMENTS

If ever there was a labour of love, it was in writing this book. It has been a hard slog researching it and the real reward has been in completing the book and leaving a lasting tribute to Hull's greatest players – every one a hero to me.

However, it would not have been possible without the help of several people and organisations, who are deserving of my thanks and appreciation.

A constant source of reference for checking my own records was Michael E. Ulyatt's *Old Faithful, A History of Hull Football Club: 1865-1987*. Bill Dalton provided the statistics for Ulyatt's book and, hopefully, we have arrived at the definitive records for each player. Credit must also be given to the late Albert Saville, who had compiled the previous Hull FC history, which formed the basis of Michael Ulyatt's book.

I spent several hours reading old files of the *Hull Daily Mail* at Hull's Central Library and both establishments earn my appreciation.

A never-ending source for cross-checking statistics is the Record Keepers' Club, through which Irving Saxton did such a marvellous job in compiling a mass of statistics. The RKC no longer exists, but the work of its former members is still greatly appreciated.

Among a number of people who provided varied amounts of information I must single out RL historian Robert Gate, who could always be relied up to produce a vital piece of detail when all seemed lost. Also, long-standing Hull supporter Claude Groizard, who added some colour to the stark career facts of players he could recall playing over seventy years ago.

For photographs, I am indebted to the editors and publishers of *League Express, Rugby League World, Rugby Leaguer, Yorkshire Post* and *Hull Daily Mail*. Individual photographers to be thanked are Andrew Varley and Andy Howard.

A special thank you to Johnny Whiteley for writing the foreword. He is truly one of the greatest of the great.

STATISTICAL NOTE

The players' records are complete to the end of 2001. They refer only to Cup and League matches plus any given official recognition by the Rugby Football League, including those against Australia and New Zealand tour squads.

The records do not include matches played before Hull joined the breakaway from the English Rugby Union in 1895, which led to the new game of rugby league. The First World War period from 1915 to 1919 is also excluded, as all games played during the war were regarded officially as friendly or charity matches.

Substitute and drop goal figures in brackets are included in the adjoining total.

FOREWORD

As I was a fan, player or coach of Hull FC for well over fifty years, the Airlie Birds have obviously been a massive part of my life. All I wanted to do when I was a youth, like many others, was to play for Hull. When I achieved my dream, I burst with pride every time I pulled on that famous black and white jersey. I was following in a long line of players who had become part of the city's sporting folklore.

I had been told stories of great players like Billy Batten, Steve Darmody and Bob Taylor, and seen for myself such men as Freddie Miller and Charlie Booth. All were my heroes and later I was to play alongside another crop of highly talented players in the 1950s. I hesitate to mention individuals because they all played their part in a marvellous era for the club. But to pack down with forwards like Mick Scott, Tommy Harris, Bob Coverdale, Harry Markham, Cyril Sykes and the Drake twins was a privilege. Then there was the incomparable Roy Francis, still a classy player when he joined Hull in his later playing years before becoming an even greater coach. Many players owe so much to him.

Although Hull went through some lean times following the successes of the 1950s, they still managed to produce a number of outstanding players – Arthur Keegan obviously comes to mind. The 1980s brought another successful era as the club bought the best available from home and overseas. Steve Norton was one of their best signings, followed by the Kiwi trio Dane O'Hara, James Leuluai and Gary Kemble.

All these, and many more, deserve some lasting recognition for the honour and service they have brought to this great club and Raymond Fletcher's book does them proud. I am pleased that Raymond, like myself an ex-Hessle Roader, has not restricted his selection to international players and record-breakers. He has also included several unsung heroes who battled on season after season, often through some of the club's grimmest times. It is right that their efforts should be recognised too.

I always regarded it as a privilege just to play for Hull. To be chosen as one of the club's '100 Greats' is an honour.

Johnny Whiteley,
March 2002

DEDICATION

To my late father, John Henry Fletcher, whose tales of the great Hull players of more than fifty years ago have stayed with me and proved an inspiration in the writing of this book.

100 HULL GREATS

Fred Ah Kuoi
Billy Anderson
George Barlow
George Bateman
Peter Bateson
Tommy Bateson**
*Billy Batten**
John 'Jack' Beasty**
Arthur Bedford
Charlie Booth**
Albert Bowers
Harold Bowman ***
Keith Boxall
Frank Boylen*
Stan Brogden
Len Casey
Eddie Caswell**
Bob Coverdale*
Mick Crane* **
*Lee Crooks**
Andy Dannatt*
Steve Darmody
Chris Davidson**
David Doyle-Davidson
Jimmy Devereux
Terry Devonshire**
Gary Divorty*
Bill Drake* **
Jim Drake*
Paul Eastwood* **
Harold Ellerington
Steve Evans*
Vince Farrar*
Cecil Fifield

Tommy Finn**
Ken Foulkes
Alf Francis
Roy Francis
Dick Gemmell*
Bert Gilbert
Emlyn Gwynne* **
Brian Hancock**
Tommy Harris ***
Jack Harrison
Karl Harrison*
Mick Harrison* **
Ernie Herbert
Tom Herridge**
Bill Holder* **
Richard Horne*
Colin Hutton
Lee Jackson*
Ernie Jenney
Mark Jones*
Arthur Keegan ***
Gary Kemble
Jim Kennedy
Paul King*
Ernie Lawrence
Charles Lempriere
James Leuluai
Sammy Lloyd
Greg Mackey
Alf Macklin**
John Maloney
Harry Markham
George Matthews
Alan McGlone

Steve McNamara*
*Freddie Miller**
Edgar Morgan*
Steve Norton ***
Dane O'Hara**
*Joe Oliver**
Paul Prendiville
Steve Prescott
Wayne Proctor*
*Ned Rogers**
Paul Rose*
Wilf Rosenberg
Bruce Ryan
*Garry Schofield**
*Mick Scott**
Trevor Skerrett*
Peter Sterling
*Billy Stone**
Charlie Stone
Clive Sullivan ***
Cyril Sykes**
Bob Taylor ***
Harry Taylor* **
Laurie Thacker**
Keith Tindall
*David Topliss**
Carl Turner**
Tevita Vaikona
George Watt
Ivor Watts**
Johnny Whiteley ***
Stan Whitty

* Great Britain Test player whilst with Hull.
** 275 or more appearances for Hull.

The top twenty players, who appear here in italics, occupy two pages instead of the usual one.

Season	Apps	Tries	Goals	Pts
1983/84	21	7	0	28
1984/85	33(3)	8	1(1)	33
1985/86	32(1)	8	0	32
1986/87	40(6)	5	0	20
TOTAL	126(10)	28	1(1)	113

Debut: v. Hull K.R. (H), 2 October 1983
Finals: Rugby League Cup 1984/85 (lost);
Yorkshire Cup 1984/85 (won), 1986/87 (lost);
John Player Trophy 1984/85 (lost)

Fred Ah Kuoi became the fourth member of New Zealand's 1980 tour squad to join Hull when he arrived at The Boulevard in 1983. Gary Kemble, Dane O'Hara and James Leuluai had already made an impact, so Ah Kuoi had a lot to live up to. In fact, he was one of the three Kiwis who agreed to join Hull in 1980, but he decided to sign for North Sydney and it was Kemble who completed the trio.

A promising player from his earliest years with Richmond, Ah Kuoi became New Zealand's youngest Test captain at twenty-two when he led them to an 18-11 victory in the third Test over the Great Britain tourists in 1979, after they had lost the first two under Graeme West's leadership. Five years later he led New Zealand to their first 3-0 Test series win against a touring Great Britain team and finished with 28 Test appearances. New Zealand won all 4 matches when Ah Kuoi was their captain.

Ah Kuoi became one of the first New Zealanders to join the exodus to the Australian Premiership when he signed for North Sydney, but struggled to command a regular place and after three years left for Hull. He did not have the best of starts with the Airlie Birds as he made his debut at stand-off in a 23-8 home defeat against the old enemy, Hull Kingston Rovers, on 2 October 1983. Injury also hampered his first season and an eight-match lay-off coincided exactly with Peter Sterling's first brief spell at Hull. After the great Australian Test star returned home, Ah Kuoi took over his scrum-half role for the rest of the season.

When Sterling returned the following season, Ah Kuoi played mostly in the centre, with David Topliss at stand-off. But Ah Kuoi was given the key midfield role alongside Sterling in two cup finals. The world-class pair teamed up to inspire Hull to a 29-12 Yorkshire Cup final defeat of Hull Kingston Rovers at Hull City's Boothferry Park and only just failed to pull off a repeat against Wigan in the memorable Rugby League Challenge Cup final at Wembley. In between those two games, Hull had lost 12-0 to Hull Kingston Rovers in the John Player final with Ah Kuoi in the centre. He was back at centre for the 1986 Yorkshire Cup final when Hull lost to Castleford.

Ah Kuoi became assistant coach to Ken Foulkes in 1986 before returning to New Zealand the following year to play for his old Auckland club, Richmond, where he ended his playing career in 1987.

Billy Anderson

Scrum-half, 1907-10, 1912-19

Season	Apps	Tries	Goals	Pts
1907/08	41	2	1	8
1908/09	39	6	4	26
1909/10	39	4	1	14
1912/13	35	2	1	8
1913/14	35	0	4	8
1914/15	29	2	2	10
1918/19	1	0	0	0
TOTAL	219	16	13	74

Debut: v. York (H), 5 September 1907
Finals: Rugby League Cup 1907/08 (lost),
1908/09 (lost), 1909/10 (drew), 1913/14 (won);
Yorkshire Cup 1912/13 (lost)

If there was ever a player who epitomised the origin of 'a good, old-fashioned scrum-half' it would be Billy Anderson. At 5ft 6in and just over 11 stone, he was a hard, wily bundle of energy, who worked closely with his forwards and provided his three-quarters with good service. His appearance and style was summed up as 'Stockings down, blood up'.

Anderson was at the heart of all four of Hull's Rugby League Challenge Cup final appearances between 1908 to 1914 and also the 1912 Yorkshire Cup final. However, it was not until the 1914 final that they won their first trophy, and that was largely due to the power of their two big international centres, Billy Batten and Bert Gilbert, stoked up by Anderson's supply of astute passes. Despite being badly hampered by a shoulder injury in the final, Anderson battled on and was the key link between forwards and backs in a move that led to Alf Francis scoring the last-minute try which clinched their 6-0 victory.

For all his consistency and value to Hull, the nearest Anderson came to gaining representa-tive honours was when he played in a 1910 tour trial, only to be overlooked for the inaugural Lions trip to Australia and New Zealand.

Born in Morecambe, Anderson crossed the country to sign for Hull in 1907 and was an immediate success, playing in all but 3 of their 44 matches that season. His debut coincided with the first appearance of two other players who were to become Hull 'Greats' – Tom Herridge and Bill Holder. The season ended with Hull reaching their first ever cup final, going down 14-0 to Hunslet in the Rugby League Challenge Cup. Anderson's craft helped them to the final in the next two seasons, only to com-plete a hat-trick of defeats.

Anderson then spent two seasons at Batley before being recalled by Hull as part of their ambitious team-building programme. By the end of the season, the great Billy Batten had been signed and Anderson was in his element with a classic three-quarter line of Alf Francis, Gilbert, Batten and Jack Harrison playing behind a big pack of forwards. It all paid off with the famous Rugby League Challenge Cup win of 1914.

He had one more full season at Hull before the First World War brought an end to com-petitive rugby for three seasons. His only game after that was in a then record 56-0 defeat at Dewsbury on 22 April 1919. It was an unfortu-nate end to the career of a player who was noted for his battling competitive spirit.

George Barlow
Hooker, 1930-42

Season	Apps	Tries	Goals	Pts
1930/31	16	1	0	3
1931/32	5	0	0	0
1932/33	10	2	0	6
1933/34	28	2	0	6
1934/35	44	4	0	12
1935/36	42	2	0	6
1936/37	34	2	0	6
1937/38	38	1	0	3
1938/39	41	0	0	0
1939/40	13	0	0	0
1940/41	0	0	0	0
1941/42	1	0	0	0
TOTAL	272	14	0	42

Debut: v. Widnes (A), 25 October 1930
Finals: Championship 1935/36 (won);
Yorkshire Cup 1938/39 (lost)

When Hull won the Championship in 1935/36 they had an outstanding back division, but they would have been much less effective without a constant supply of possession. The man who supplied it was George Barlow, a top-class hooker of the old school. In the days when there were over fifty scrums per match, Barlow usually got more than his fair share. He also had a heavy workload in the loose, particularly in defence.

Barlow's steady consistency made him a fixture in the Hull pack as he averaged around 40 matches per season in the five years before the outbreak of the Second World War. But for that interruption, he would have made well over 300 appearances for Hull. As it was, he made only a handful of appearances over the next few years, when he would have been at his peak.

Vital as Barlow was to Hull's plans, his unspectacular solid performances were not the type to hit the headlines. Yet his name will always be synonymous with one of the most talked about matches played at The Boulevard – because he was sent off. His dismissal came in the closing minutes of a fierce 1936 Rugby League Challenge Cup third round battle with Leeds before Hull's biggest home crowd of 28,798 (still a record). Barlow was sent off for a foul on Leeds centre Fred Harris and was followed by Hull captain Joe Oliver for dissent. The match finished in uproar as Leeds scraped a 5-4 victory.

Later that year, Barlow was the hero as one of his rare tries proved vital in Hull's 17-13 Yorkshire Cup first round defeat of Hull Kingston Rovers in a typically hard-fought derby battle.

Barlow's only representative appearance came in 1934/35 when he played for Yorkshire at Headingley. Even then the honour was curtailed as the match was abandoned after forty-five minutes because of adverse weather conditions. The 5-5 result was allowed to stand. His brief county career was scant recognition for a player who gave Hull tremendous service.

Barlow's brother, Laurie, played over 170 matches in the 1930s and the pair packed down together many times, including in the 1936 Championship final.

George Bateman
Winger, 1930-35

Season	Apps	Tries	Goals	Pts
1930/31	32	30	0	90
1931/32	38	28	0	84
1932/33	27	17	0	51
1933/34	29	21	0	63
1934/35	43	26	0	78
1935/36	10	4	0	12
TOTAL	179	126	0	378

Debut: v. Featherstone R. (H),
20 September 1930 (1 try)

Only a few players divided a long and successful playing career almost equally between Hull and Hull Kingston Rovers. One of them was George Bateman. The locally-born winger scored 65 tries in five seasons with Rovers and then crossed the city to score 126 in just over five seasons at Hull.

Hull signed him soon after he finished as Rovers' top tryscorer with 21 in 1929/30, and at the end of his first season with the Airlie Birds, he headed their try chart with 30. In fact, Bateman was Hull's leading tryscorer in all but one of his five full seasons at the club. Rovers' fans' dismay at Bateman's signing for their rivals grew as he seemed to take extra delight in scoring against his old club. It began with the Christmas Day derby battle a few months after he had swapped sides when he scored both tries in an 8-2 victory. Bateman might have forgotten much of what happened during the match as he sustained concussion in a collision with Rovers' George Saddington, but he produced a reminder in the Good Friday return game as he scored Hull's only try in an 11-5 defeat. He went on to

total eight tries for Hull in derby matches.

Hull Kingston Rovers had signed the former Coldstream Guardsman in 1925 after he had scored over 100 tries in army rugby union and also played for the Surrey county side.

Although the 1930s was an era of great wingers, such as Alf Ellaby and Eric Harris, Bateman twice finished in the season's top ten tryscorers' list. His highest finish was sixth in 1930/31 when he totalled 32 tries, including two for Yorkshire. He had scored a try on his debut for Hull, and although Hull struggled to hold a mid-table position, Bateman continued to run in tries and finished with a scoring burst of 18 in their last 14 matches, including another hat-trick and a four-try romp in a 21-12 defeat of Batley.

Despite his prolific scoring rate, Bateman's only representative honours as a Hull player came with just 4 appearances for Yorkshire. He maintained his impressive average to score four tries for the county, but the nearest he got to attaining higher honours came in 1932 when he played in a tour trial. However, there was no call-up for the trip to Australasia and Bateman went back to rattling in the tries for Hull, finishing with a career total of 126 that puts him in ninth in their all-time list.

He played his last game for Hull in the centre at Keighley on 16 November 1935. Ironically, after never reaching a final during Bateman's six years at the club, Hull finished the season as Champions with the defeat of Widnes in the play-off final.

Peter Bateson

Full-back, 1957-62

Season	Apps	Tries	Goals	Pts
1957/58	35	1	131	265
1958/59	22	0	99	198
1959/60	38	2	161	328
1960/61	23	2	85	176
1961/62	20	0	66	132
TOTAL	138	5	542	1099

Debut: v. Leeds (H), 17 August 1957 (7 goals)
Finals: Championship 1957/58 (won, 4 goals);
Yorkshire Cup 1959/60 (lost, 4 goals)

Peter Bateson earns a place among Hull FC's elite mainly for his 542 goals, which place him fifth in their all-time list of kickers. His tally of just five tries correctly suggests he was not the most attack-minded of full-backs, but they helped make him the club's seventh most prolific pointscorer with 1,099 in only five seasons.

Although Hull-born, he turned professional with Batley and had four seasons there before departing for Australia. Hull got their man when he returned a year later.

Bateson's first season at Hull was probably his best, culminating with him kicking four goals in the 20-3 Championship final defeat of Workington Town in 1958. He had also earned a place in one of the tour trial matches. But despite kicking seven goals in the Whites' 41-18 victory at Headingley, the Great Britain tour selectors chose his opposite number, Eric Fraser, plus Glyn Moses.

He was also unlucky to miss two Wembley appearances. After playing in the previous two rounds of the Rugby League Challenge Cup in 1959, including kicking three goals in the 15-5 semi-final defeat of Featherstone Rovers, Bateson lost his cup final place to the promising young Arthur Keegan.

That was fair enough, but a cruel blow cost him a Wembley appearance a year later. He had totalled two tries and kicked 14 goals, including a drop goal, in the four previous rounds before disaster struck the week before Wembley. Hull were playing their cup final opponents, Wakefield Trinity, in a Championship play-off semi-final when Bateson was felled by a late, off-the-ball tackle by Derek Turner. Bateson was carried off suffering from severe concussion. He was ruled out of the final and never fully recovered from the blow as a player.

Although Hull reached the cup semi-final again a year later, Bateson declared he did not want to play any more that season as he did not want to risk another injury. He pointed out that it was a question of insurance rather than actual fear of being injured that prompted his decision.

Bateson resumed playing the following season, struggled to retain his first-team place and two years later returned to Batley before retiring in September 1964.

Tommy Bateson

Second row, 1923-31

Season	Apps	Tries	Goals	Pts
1923/24	18	6	2	22
1924/25	37	7	19	59
1925/26	44	6	50	118
1926/27	37	15	50	145
1927/28	43	10	41	112
1928/29	38	16	31	110
1929/30	32	9	38	103
1930/31	33	3	11	31
TOTAL	282	72	242	700

Debut: v. Hull K.R. (H), 29 September 1923
Finals: Yorkshire Cup 1927/28 (lost)

Although Tommy Bateson made his debut for Hull in the centre, it was as a back-row forward that he made a big impression in the 1920s. He would probably have been a good centre, but he stood out in the pack with his all-round ability that brought him a steady stream of tries and well over 200 goals.

Christened Arnold, but popularly known as Tommy, he gave Hull good service for several seasons and reached a peak in 1927/28 when he was rated one of the best forwards in the country. All of his three representative appearances came that season as he played in each of Yorkshire's matches at loose forward. Although Yorkshire won only once, Bateson made his mark by scoring in all three with a total of five goals and a try. He also maintained a steady scoring rate for Hull to finish in the season's top ten list, just as he had done the year before.

Bateson's impressive form earned him a place in one of the two tour trials in 1928, but he failed to gain selection for the trip to Australia and New Zealand. There were some who thought he deserved selection at least as much as club forward colleague Harold Bowman, who was selected along with Hull winger Emlyn Gwynne.

The loose forward had also been unlucky in the Yorkshire Cup final early that season when he was in the side that lost 7-2 to Dewsbury at Headingley. It was his only cup final appearance as Hull struggled to regain the consistency that had brought them so much success in the early part of the 1920s. Despite his lack of medals and few representative honours, Bateson always gained plenty of respect from opposition forwards with greater reputations.

Bateson's debut for Hull was against arch rivals Hull Kingston Rovers and after being in the centre and away from the close quarter confrontations, he relished the derby battles more when he moved into the forwards. Of the 14 matches he played against Rovers, perhaps the keenest were when he faced Jack Feetham, one of the East Hull side's greatest loose forwards. There was never a lot to choose between them, although Feetham went on to tour Down Under with Great Britain and play in eight Test matches, most of these taking place after his transfer to Salford.

Always regarded as a fit, full 80 minutes forward, Bateson suffered ill-health in later life and died in 1960 after a long illness, aged just fifty-eight.

Billy Batten
Centre, 1913-24

Season	Apps	Tries	Goals	Pts
1912/13	3	4	0	12
1913/14	29	10	1	32
1914/15	24	5	0	15
1918/19	14	17	0	51
1919/20	35	21	0	63
1920/21	23	15	0	45
1921/22	35	8	0	24
1922/23	35	6	0	18
1923/24	28	3	0	9
TOTAL	226	89	1	269

Debut: v. Keighley (H), 12 April 1913 (3 tries)
Finals: Rugby League Cup 1913/14 (won),
1921/22 (lost, 1 try); Championship 1919/20
(won, 1 try), 1920/21 (won); Yorkshire Cup
1914/15 (lost), 1920/21 (lost), 1923/24 (lost, 1 try)

The Greatest of the Greats. No other Hull player is held in such high esteem as Billy Batten. As an original member of the RFL Hall of Fame, Batten's reputation is recognised throughout the game. In a twenty-year career, which took place during the first quarter of the twentieth century, he was a superstar long before the word was coined. His shock move from Hunslet to Hull in April 1913 caused a sensation with the £600 transfer fee doubling the previous world record.

It is popularly believed that he was paid a then amazing £14 per match, but he said at the time of his signing for Hull: 'They have agreed to pay me the equivalent of £4 per week all the year round. Hunslet never paid me more than 50s for a win. Others make £4 a week in the Northern Union game, so why shouldn't I?' He added that soccer's Manchester United had offered him £4 a week two years earlier, such was his all-round sporting ability.

Although he played most of his Test rugby on the wing, Batten was best known as a powerful centre. Rather than go round a player, he would prefer to go through him – or over him with one of his famed leaps. The leap was eventually banned, but Batten remained a difficult man to bring down because of his knees-up style of running. He was equally fearsome in defence, mastering a smother tackle that one opponent said was like being hit by a ton of coal. Above all, he was a winger's centre. He may have scored a hat-trick on his Hull debut, but he regarded sending his winger away as his main job.

Playing colleague Jim Kennedy once said: 'Billy would say that if there was no chance of the winger doing anything with the ball, he would take the hammer himself. Yet, when he let you have the ball, it was a beautiful pass.'

Born in Kinsley, near Pontefract, Batten began his senior career with Hunslet and made his Test debut against New Zealand in 1908, three months before he was nineteen. The teenager was also a member of the Hunslet team that became the first to win all four cups in a season. By the time he joined Hull he was already a major star, but he became an even greater idol at The Boulevard. Yet he almost went to rivals Hull Kingston Rovers, who put in a record-breaking bid before Hull came up with an even bigger one.

It was to prove money well spent as his arrival began one of the most glorious eras in the club's

BATTEN IN TRAINING AT HULL CATTLE MARKET

How cartoonist Ern Shaw depicted Billy Batten preparing for a big cup tie.

history. Hull had never won a trophy before Batten joined them, losing a succession of finals. During his time at the club they won the lot, including the Rugby League Challenge Cup at the end of his first full season with them. In the 1920 Championship final, it was Batten's powerful charge for the line that gave the Airlie Birds a 3-2 victory over Huddersfield and brought the title to Hull for the first time.

It was not a one-man team, of course, and Batten formed one of the greatest club centre partnerships of all time alongside Bert Gilbert, the Australian Test player, who had been signed a year earlier. But Batten was the fans' big favourite and when he was awarded a benefit match in 1920, it produced another financial record, with the centre receiving a cheque for £1,080. He had four more years at Hull before transferring to Wakefield Trinity for £350 in May 1924.

Within two years he had helped Wakefield to two Yorkshire Cup final victories, the last coming nineteen years after he had received his first winner's medal with Hunslet. He moved on to Castleford and played just eight times before retiring after his last match at Hull Kingston Rovers on 9 April 1927. He was thirty-eight.

Surprisingly, Batten only made one of his 10 appearances for Great Britain as a Hull player. This was due to the outbreak of the First World

War and also his refusal to play in trial matches to test his fitness after injuries that ruled him out of the 1914 and 1920 tours to Australasia. He had toured in 1910 while he was at Hunslet. Batten played four times for England during his years at Hull and made four appearances for Yorkshire. He also captained both country and county.

Batten's career ran parallel with Huddersfield's Harold Wagstaff, another legendary centre and Hall of Fame member. Yet they never formed a centre partnership for Great Britain. In opposition they were great rivals, although respectful of each other. It was always regarded as Wagstaff's class against Batten's power, but the latter was also a clever player with skills to match most of his contemporaries.

Batten's son, Eric, followed him as an outstanding winger with Hunslet, Bradford Northern and Featherstone Rovers. He also toured Australasia and played for Great Britain, while Billy's grandson Ray Batten gained Test honours as Leeds' loose forward. Two other sons, Billy Jnr and Bob, also played professional rugby league.

A fitness fanatic, Batten kept in good trim until he was severely injured when struck on the head by heavy roof tiles while working at Hemsworth. He was sixty years old and after a spell in hospital became an invalid for the next ten years before dying in January 1959.

Season	Apps	Tries	Goals	Pts
1912/13	1	0	0	0
1913/14	1	0	0	0
1914/15	12	1	0	3
1918/19	11	1	0	3
1919/20	27	2	0	6
1920/21	33	3	0	9
1921/22	40	3	0	9
1922/23	32	1	0	3
1923/24	33	1	0	3
1924/25	26	0	0	0
1925/26	42	0	0	0
1926/27	25	1	0	3
TOTAL	283	13	0	39

Debut: v. Huddersfield (A), 25 December 1912
Finals: Rugby League Cup 1921/22 (lost),
1922/23 (lost); Championship 1920/21 (won);
Yorkshire Cup 1920/21 (lost), 1923/24 (won)

It used to be said that forwards were labourers for the backs. If that were true, then none laboured harder or much longer than John Beasty. During Hull's first glorious era over eighty years ago many great three-quarters played for the Airlie Birds, including the legendary Billy Batten plus flying wingers Alf Francis and Billy Stone. They grabbed all the headlines, but without the likes of Beasty doing the hard graft up front, their opportunities would have been limited.

From 1912 onwards, Beasty was there match after match for the best part of fourteen years, in the engine room that provided the team's power. Those were the days when front-row forwards had to work hard in the scrums to win possession and then do overtime in the loose. Beasty did that for 283 matches and the total would have been far greater had the First World War not robbed him of three competitive seasons. A mere 13 tries in fourteen years are an indication of where his selfless priorities lay.

He was the archetypal unsung hero. Neither county nor international honours came his way. Yet Hull relied on him heavily, particularly during the first half of the 1920s when they challenged strongly for all the trophies. Beasty was the cornerstone of the pack that laid the foundations for Hull's Championship win in 1920/21, and eleven years after making his debut he helped them win the Yorkshire Cup for the first time in 1923.

Sometimes called Jack, but popularly known as Johnno, Beasty made his debut at Huddersfield on Christmas Day 1912. A local lad, he was given the opportunity when Hull rested a few players because they had a big derby battle with Hull Kingston Rovers the following day. It was his only appearance of the season, but once he had become a first-team regular, he was one of the few players Hull did not rest, no matter how crowded their fixtures. In 1921 he was the only player to appear in all 10 of Hull's matches in the last twenty-nine days of the season, including the 10-9 Rugby League Challenge Cup final defeat by Rochdale Hornets. It seemed that Hull just could not do without him.

Arthur Bedford

Second row, 1946-55

Season	Apps	Tries	Goals	Pts
1946/47	25	2	0	6
1947/48	27	3	0	9
1948/49	11	0	0	0
1949/50	33	2	0	6
1950/51	32	2	0	6
1951/52	34	8	0	24
1952/53	11	2	0	6
1953/54	24	2	0	6
1954/55	10	0	0	0
1955/56	1	0	0	0
TOTAL	208	21	0	63

Debut: v. Castleford (H), 5 September 1946
Finals: Yorkshire Cup 1953/54 (lost)

A veteran at twenty-five. That was the doubtful description of Arthur Bedford in 1952, but it was meant as a well-deserved tribute. For second-rower Bedford was then the oldest forward in a young Hull pack that was to become a feared force throughout the rest of the 1950s. Although Bedford was not to share in Hull's success of the latter half of the decade, he played a major role in the pack's formative years. Future international forwards such as Mick Scott, Tommy Harris and Johnny Whiteley all benefited from his experience.

Bedford, whose brother Ted also played for Hull, had already made over 100 appearances when the rich crop of young forward talent started arriving. He was still young himself, of course, and under coach Roy Francis's guidance, Bedford played a leading role. With a dashing cavalier style, his enthusiasm was infectious and he always looked as if he was enjoying himself while taking his pack responsibilities very seriously. Even when Hull were overwhelmed 28-0 by the 1952 Australian side, the *Hull Daily Mail* reported: 'Bedford fought like a hero'.

A local dock-worker, like others in the pack, Bedford signed for Hull and quickly gained a regular first-team place. The early post-war years were difficult for Hull as they sought to rebuild both on and off the field. While a number of pre-war players resumed playing for Hull, the club's future lay with the likes of Bedford, whose style was fast making him a big favourite with The Boulevard supporters. Although Bedford gained no representative honours, he maintained a high level of consistency until the promising young back-row forwards he had helped to bring along began to replace him.

His only Cup final appearance came when Hull lost 7-2 to Bradford Northern in the 1953 Yorkshire Cup final. Despite the defeat Hull's future looked promising, as the mighty pack was now almost complete. Bedford would shortly have to make way for Bill Drake, but he could take pride in being in at the beginning.

Bedford's service was rewarded when he was granted a joint benefit with Ivor Watts in 1955. With the young forwards he had nurtured now keeping him out of the first team, Hull also granted him a free transfer and he moved to Hull Kingston Rovers in December 1956. His last game for Hull was at home to Leeds on 24 September 1955.

Charlie Booth

Second row, 1935-50

Season	Apps	Tries	Goals	Pts
1935/36	36	7	0	21
1936/37	30	5	0	15
1937/38	38	6	0	18
1938/39	41	3	0	9
1939/40	30	8	0	24
1940/41	12	3	0	9
1941/42	3	0	0	0
1942/43	1	0	0	0
1943/44	6	1	0	3
1944/45	19	3	0	9
1945/46	35	3	0	9
1946/47	30	4	0	12
1947/48	34	3	0	9
1948/49	18	1	1	5
1949/50	3	0	0	0
TOTAL	336	47	1	143

Debut: v. Keighley (H), 31 August 1935 (1 try)
Finals: Championship 1935/36 (won);
Yorkshire Cup 1938/39 (lost), 1946/47 (lost)

Only six forwards played more times for Hull than Charlie Booth, and his total of 336 appearances would have been far greater had he not been restricted to only 22 matches over four wartime seasons. Before the Second World War he had established himself as a regular in a strong Hull pack that included internationals Laurie Thacker and Harold Ellerington, and he was still packing down in the first team four years after the war.

The young Booth was a champion right from the start of his senior career. He scored a try on his debut in the first match of the 1935/36 season and finished the campaign with a Championship-winning medal after helping Hull beat Widnes 21-2 in the final. There was an additional medal, too, as Hull also won the Yorkshire League.

He was not so lucky in 1938 when Hull went down 18-10 to Huddersfield in the Yorkshire Cup final or in the 1946 county final when Wakefield Trinity beat them 10-0. Booth was one of only three Hull players to play in the two county finals spanning the war years.

A big, black-haired, beetle-browed forward, he seemed almost indestructible in the days when forward battles were like trench warfare. Yet off the field, although he worked on the docks, he did not look like a typical rugby league forward as he wore large horn-rimmed, bottle-glass spectacles. Without them he had poor vision and there is a popular story that claims he once broke through and touched down over the 25-yard line.

He played mostly in the second row until moving to prop in his last few seasons, when his vast experience was invaluable in bringing along a new crop of young Hull forwards.

Booth's three appearances for England all came before 1940, with the outbreak of war interrupting a career that would probably have brought more honours. He did tour France with a Northern XIII squad in 1937/38 and played a total of five matches for Yorkshire before and after the war.

Booth played his last match for Hull at home to Dewsbury on 22 April 1950 and took over as the A-team trainer. Two sons, Charlie and Roger, also played for Hull in the 1960s.

Albert Bowers

Winger, 1938-48

Season	Apps	Tries	Goals	Pts
1938/39	22	5	0	15
1939/40	26	24	0	72
1940/41	1	1	0	3
1941/42	4	3	0	9
1942/43	0	0	0	0
1943/44	0	0	0	0
1944/45	3	1	0	3
1945/46	31	14	0	42
1946/47	30	14	0	42
1947/48	34	16	0	48
1948/49	11	4	0	12
TOTAL	162	82	0	246

Debut: v. Warrington (H), 26 November 1938
Finals: Yorkshire Cup 1946/47 (lost)

Many players throughout the game lost their best playing years to the Second World War and one of the worst hit was Albert Bowers. Signed by Hull from local amateur rugby league in 1937, the young Bowers soon showed he was a winger of real potential. In only his second season he finished third in the try chart with 24 in 26 matches. The only players ahead of him were international wingers Eric Batten (38 tries) of Hunslet and Bradford Northern's Emlyn Walters (25). But the season was 1939/40 and it had begun just a week before the outbreak of war.

Although Bowers was a first-team regular throughout that War Emergency League campaign, it was to be his last full season until peace returned. In the five remaining wartime seasons he managed only eight appearances and scored just four tries.

He was back on the wing for most of Hull's first post-war season, scoring 14 tries for a side that struggled around mid-table. The following year Hull signed brilliant Australian left-winger Bruce Ryan, and with Bowers on the right they formed a formidable pair, albeit with contrasting styles. Ryan was a superbly-built athlete full of confidence, while Bowers was of much lighter stature with the nervous edge of a top-class sprinter. And while Ryan's strong build allowed him to come inside with great effect, Bowers preferred to play the touchline and beat his opposite number on the outside with pace.

In an era of outstanding wingers, Bowers twice appeared for England and was considered a shade unlucky not to be selected for Great Britain in at least one of the three 1947 Test matches against New Zealand. He had pushed his claims strongly with two tries for England against Wales a fortnight before the third Test. But it was the Wales right-winger, Roy Francis, who got the Test call. In fairness, Francis, who was to become one of Hull's all-time greats, did justify his Test selection with two tries in the Great Britain victory.

Bowers also played twice for Yorkshire, picking up a County Championship winners' medal in 1946. The only medal he received playing for Hull was a losers' one after they lost 10-0 to Wakefield Trinity in the Yorkshire Cup final at Headingley the same year.

Harold Bowman

Prop, 1921-34

Season	Apps	Tries	Goals	Pts
1921/22	4	0	0	0
1922/23	40	5	0	15
1923/24	31	3	0	9
1924/25	24	3	0	9
1925/26	44	16	0	48
1926/27	40	8	0	24
1927/28	45	2	0	6
1928/29	33	6	0	18
1929/30	39	6	0	18
1930/31	41	5	0	15
1931/32	34	6	0	18
1932/33	31	9	0	27
1933/34	41	6	0	18
1934/35	4	0	0	0
TOTAL	**451**	**75**	**0**	**225**

Debut: v. Halifax (H), 10 December 1921
Finals: Rugby League Cup 1922/23 (lost);
Yorkshire Cup 1923/24 (won), 1927/28 (lost)

From a rather delicate schoolboy to a mighty prop forward who twice toured Australia and New Zealand with Great Britain in the 1920s; that was the remarkable transformation of Harold Bowman. Brought up in the heart of Hull's industrial area, he was only thirteen when failing health caused his parents to send him into the country to work on a farm. It did the trick and as a rapidly growing youth he became a fine all-round sportsman, excelling at cycling and running.

He also played village soccer for North Newbald and such was his impressive build and enthusiasm that former Hull international full-back Harry Taylor thought he had what it takes to be a rugby player. Following his suggestion, young Bowman was invited down to The Boulevard for trials. They were suitably impressed, and at nineteen he made his first-team debut in December 1921.

Although props usually take time to gain much-needed experience, Bowman made rapid progress and after gaining county honours for Yorkshire, he was only twenty-two when selected for the 1924 tour of Australasia, having impressed in two trial matches.

Along with club colleague Stan Whitty, they became the first Hull-born players to go on tour and Bowman marked it with 12 appearances, including two Test matches. He toured again four years later and would have made it a record three tours by a forward, but after playing in a trial match he decided against making the 1932 trip.

His international career included 8 Test appearances, 4 matches for England and 13 for Yorkshire. There was no doubt he was one of the best forwards of his era, with a total of more than 90 tries in club and representative games quite exceptional for a prop, especially in those days.

He was in particularly rampaging form in 1925/26 when he was one of Hull's top tryscorers with 16 for the club plus a try for Yorkshire. Although he was always in the thick of play, he had a remarkable run of

Harold Bowman dives over for a try.

consistency. In 1927/28 he played in all but 4 of Hull's 49 matches.

Bowman never wanted to play for any other club but Hull and stayed with them throughout his fourteen-year career. He captained them for a while and when he retired in 1934 he had played in a total of 451 first-team matches, which places him third in Hull's all-time list of career appearances.

After his playing career ended, he led a busy and eventful life as a farmer at Holme on Spalding Moor, and a publican at Pocklington, where he had a fish and chip shop and a turf accountancy business.

Twenty years after retiring as a player, he would be proud to see his son, Keith, playing on the wing for Hull after being transferred from Hunslet. Later Harold's grandson, Chris Bowman, made quite an impact as a tryscoring prop for Bramley. Sadly, Keith was in the dressing room as a reserve for a 1957 Championship semi-final match against Barrow at Hull City's Boothferry Park when he was told his father had collapsed in the stand and died. He was only fifty-five.

Although Bowman's 5ft 10in and 14st statistics would be modest enough for a prop now, in the 1920s they were regarded as the ideal build for a front-row forward. Add an aggressive approach and it made him one of the most feared forwards of his day. He was fortunate that in his early days he packed down with some of Hull's greatest forwards of all-time, including fellow members of the *100 Greats* elite John Beasty, Edgar Morgan and Bob Taylor. Their experience rubbed off on young Bowman, and at the end of his first full season, he packed down with them in the Rugby League Challenge Cup final against Leeds. However, it was yet another final in which Hull failed to do themselves justice and they crashed to a 28-3 defeat.

Bowman's only winner's medal from three finals came with the 10-4 defeat of Huddersfield in 1923, when Hull won the Yorkshire Cup for the first time. But although trophies were hard to come by, he remained one of the top forwards in the game throughout the 1920s and shared in two Great Britain Ashes triumphs.

Keith Boxall

Second row, 1970-81

Season	Apps	Tries	Goals	Pts
1969/70	6(1)	0	0	0
1970/71	39(2)	14	31	104
1971/72	42(1)	12	14	64
1972/73	35(2)	5	36	87
1973/74	4(2)	0	0	0
1974/75	27(2)	4	34	80
1975/76	31(2)	21	58	179
1976/77	37	20	15	90
1977/78	36(1)	11	19	71
1978/79	16(10)	4	0	12
1979/80	30(7)	7	0	21
1980/81	17(6)	0	0	0
TOTAL	320(36)	98	207	708

Debut: v. Dewsbury (A), 28 March 1970
Finals: Player's No. 6 Trophy 1975/76 (lost, 2
goals); BBC Floodlit Trophy 1979/80 (won)

He was not your classic second-row forward, but Keith Boxall ran with devastating effect in the mid-1970s. Nicknamed 'Rhino' because of his mighty charges, Boxall totalled over 40 tries in the two seasons when Second Division Hull were surprise Player's No. 6 Trophy finalists and then promoted Champions. Although he was short and stocky for a second-row forward, with his blond hair and rumbling runs he stood out in a pack that dominated the Second Division.

In 1975/76 his 21 touchdowns put him ninth in the try chart as the top tryscoring forward. He also banged over 58 goals, making him a key figure in a side that was emerging from the depressing early years of the decade. One of his best performances that season was in the shock 22-14 victory in the Player's No. 6 Trophy semi-final at Salford, who went on to become First Division Champions. Boxall seemed almost unstoppable as he burst through for two tries. He maintained his form the following promotion season when he scored 20 tries and played in all 37 League and cup matches.

Boxall carried his form into county matches and scored a try in two of his three appearances for Yorkshire. A local lad, Boxall was signed from East Mount Youth Club in 1968 and soon became a regular in Hull's first team before injury restricted him to only four appearances in 1973/74. Once back to full fitness, he hit his best form and became a firm favourite with the fans, especially those in the Threepenny Stand.

Boxall maintained a high level of consistency throughout a decade in which Hull's fortunes fluctuated widely. He battled through the first few years when Hull hit one of the worst periods in their history, enjoyed some of the success of the mid-1970s and shared in the 1979 BBC Floodlit Trophy defeat of Hull Kingston Rovers. Unfortunately, his career was coming to an end when Hull started on their glory days of the 1980s, and he played his last match in March 1981.

23

Frank Boylen

Prop/second row, 1908-12

Season	Apps	Tries	Goals	Pts
1908/09	39	7	1	23
1909/10	28	4	0	12
1910/11	33	1	1	5
1911/12	37	2	0	6
1912/13	5	0	0	0
TOTAL	142	14	2	46

Debut: v. Bradford N. (H), 3 September 1908
Finals: Rugby League Cup 1908/09 (lost)

As the first Hull player to be selected for a Great Britain tour of Australia and New Zealand, Frank Boylen has a special place in the club's history. The tour call came in 1910 when he had already made his mark with two other notable firsts for club and country. A prominent rugby union forward with Hartlepool Rovers and Durham, Boylen played in all four international matches for England early in 1908 before switching codes and signing for Hull. Just eleven months after playing in his last rugby union international and with fewer than 30 appearances in the 13-a-side game, Boylen was playing for Great Britain against Australia.

It made him the first Hull player to play against the Kangaroos in a Test match and the first former England rugby union international to play for Great Britain. While reports suggested Boylen was the pick of the British pack, which laid the foundations for a 6-5 third Test win that made them the first Ashes winners, it was to be Boylen's only appearance for Great Britain.

But he continued with his good form for Hull and at the end of his first momentous season he played in the Rugby League Challenge Cup final against Wakefield Trinity. Although Hull were beaten 17-0, Boylen had made extraordinary progress and a year later he was rewarded with a place in the first Great Britain squad to tour Down Under in 1910. Boylen notched up a less distinguished first when he was sent off in the match against Metropolis – the first Great Britain tourist to be dismissed. Jack Hickey of Metropolis was also sent off and the disciplinary officials set an international trend by letting off both players with a caution. Boylen played seven matches on tour, scoring a try and kicking five goals.

Back at home, his popularity with the Hull supporters rose on Boxing Day that year when he scored the converted try that gave the Airlie Birds a 5-5 draw at Hull Kingston Rovers. It was a rare touchdown for the prop or second row regarded as a hard, grafting forward rather than the breakaway type. Known as Patsy since his rugby union days, Boylen's progress in rugby league was all the more remarkable in that he was twenty-nine when he turned professional. In contrast, Harold Havelock, a rugby union colleague who signed for Hull at the same time, never made the grade and played only 31 matches for the club.

In addition to his Test appearance, Boylen played three times for England and made four appearances for Yorkshire while with Hull. He moved to York in 1912, taking over as captain, and had non-competitive wartime spells back at Hull and Hull Kingston Rovers, with whom he continued in peacetime.

Stan Brogden
Centre, 1938-45

Season	Apps	Tries	Goals	Pts
1938/39	29	14	0	42
1939/40	3	0	0	0
1940/41	18	9	5	37
1941/42	15	5	0	15
1942/43	11	2	6	18
1943/44	0	0	0	0
1944/45	8	3	8	25
TOTAL	84	33	19	137

Debut: v. Castleford (A), 17 September 1938

The war prevented Hull from getting full value from Stan Brogden after they signed him from Leeds in 1938 for a then considerable £1,200. He had been one of the outstanding players of the 1930s, playing 16 times for Great Britain and making two tours of Australia and New Zealand. Blessed with terrific pace and natural ability, the only question mark against him was regarding his best position – wing, centre or stand-off? He played all three roles for Britain.

Brogden had made his senior rugby league debut at seventeen for Bradford Northern in April 1927 and was still a teenager when transferred to Huddersfield for a record-equalling £1,000 two years later. Leeds broke the record when they signed him for £1,200 in March 1934 and he had four great years there before Hull paid a similar sum to lure him to The Boulevard. He thus became the first player to be transferred for £1,000 or more three times.

At twenty-eight he still had several good years ahead of him and they started off well enough, although his signing came too late to be registered for the Yorkshire Cup and he missed out on Hull's county final defeat against Huddersfield. Brogden finished his first season at Hull as their leading try scorer with 14, playing all but one of his 29 matches in the centre. Representative honours also continued to come his way with two appearances at centre for Yorkshire and one on the wing for England.

After playing in the first two matches of the following term, war broke out and Brogden managed only one appearance in the Emergency League season. Although war ruled out Great Britain's scheduled tour Down Under in the summer, Brogden played centre and scored two tries in a 1936 Tourists team v. 1940 Tour Probables match, suggesting that he would have made the trip to Australasia. Altogether he played four times for England and thrice for Yorkshire as a Hull player, but his appearances for the Airlie Birds continued to be irregular during wartime.

The glimpses Hull fans did get of him were enough for them to appreciate what a great asset he would have been in peace-time. As a competitive sprinter, he retained much of his speed well into the veteran stage. This enabled him to still beat much younger players with a body swerve or his famed 'corkscrew' run.

He was thirty-four when he left Hull, but his career was far from over as he had spells with Rochdale Hornets and Salford before joining the newly-formed Whitehaven in 1948 for his twenty-second and last season. Brogden was at stand-off when the Cumbrians played their first game – and beat Hull 5-0.

Len Casey

Second row/loose forward, 1970-75

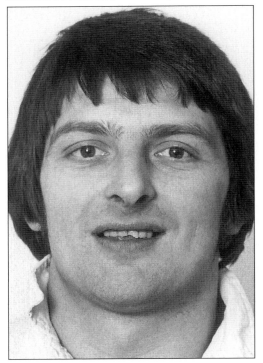

Season	Apps	Tries	Goals	Pts
1970/71	7(3)	4	0	12
1971/72	4(2)	0	0	0
1972/73	31(7)	2	0	6
1973/74	30(1)	6	0	18
1974/75	27	2	0	6
1975/76	6	0	0	0
TOTAL	105(13)	16	0	42

Debut: v. Keighley (A), 9 September 1970

Although Len Casey's greatest days occurred after he left The Boulevard, he first made a big impression as a tough-tackling back-row forward with Hull. A local junior, Casey scored a try in each of his first four matches for Hull and was soon being tipped as a future star. His five formative years with Hull were during one of their grimmest periods, as they struggled in the lower regions of the old one league and then in the Second Division.

'Cast Iron' Casey, as he became known, made the most of it before deciding he was ready to move up. His fans could have accepted that, but it came as a shock when the West Hull lad crossed the city to join arch rivals Hull Kingston Rovers in 1975. The fee was £6,000 and his rapid progress was reflected in subsequent transfers as he moved on to Bradford Northern in a £25,000 deal in 1979 before returning to Rovers just thirteen months later for a then world record fee of £38,000.

Casey achieved great success with Bradford and Rovers, making 14 appearances for Great Britain, including two as captain. He went on Britain's tour of Australasia in 1979 and was selected for the 1984 trip, but was withdrawn after he was banned for six months. The suspension followed his pushing of a touch judge after he had been sent off playing for Hull Kingston Rovers in a typical derby battle against Hull.

Casey played in other memorable derby clashes against Hull, including Rovers' 1980 Wembley victory and their 1981 Premiership Final win when he was awarded the Harry Sunderland Trophy as the Man of the Match.

His playing career ended with a spell as Wakefield Trinity's player-coach, making seven appearances at the beginning of the 1985/86 season as he steered them to promotion. Then, after eleven years, he returned to The Boulevard as Hull's coach in June 1986. Less than two years later he suddenly quit – just two weeks before a Rugby League Challenge Cup semi-final. He claimed the board was impossible to work with and his resignation was also in support of full-back Paul Fletcher, who was in a contract dispute.

Casey later became a Hull Kingston Rovers director and then took over as Scarborough Pirates' coach but was sacked halfway through their one season of 1991/92.

Eddie Caswell
Scrum-half, 1919-31

Season	Apps	Tries	Goals	Pts
1919/20	17	5	0	15
1920/21	38	10	0	30
1921/22	42	17	1	53
1922/23	43	24	0	72
1923/24	40	13	0	39
1924/25	35	6	0	18
1925/26	44	10	3	36
1926/27	44	5	0	15
1927/28	49	4	0	12
1928/29	19	3	0	9
1929/30	25	1	1	5
1930/31	5	0	0	0
TOTAL	401	98	5	304

Debut: v. Batley (A), 25 October 1919
Finals: Rugby League Cup 1921/22 (lost),
1922/23 (lost); Championship 1920/21 (won);
Yorkshire Cup 1920/21 (lost), 1923/24 (won),
1927/28 (lost)

There have been many players described as 'One of the best never to play for Great Britain'. But few deserved the accolade more than Eddie Caswell, especially when referring to scrum-halves. In a decade of outstanding No.7s during the 1920s, headed by the great Jonty Parkin, Caswell was often on the fringe of Test honours without quite making it. His only representative appearances were three matches for Wales and one for Glamorgan and Monmouthshire.

Signed from the Cardiff Rugby Union Club, Caswell had only a short settling-in period before becoming a firm favourite at The Boulevard. Small, but powerfully built, he looked a natural for the rugby league game. He was soon working the blind side like an old master, and with his dazzling sidestep plus the cheekiest of dummies, he tormented the opposition to distraction.

Caswell was also a superb ball-player, who brought the best out of his forwards and none benefited more than Bob Taylor. The massive second-row forward joined Hull a couple of months after Caswell's debut, and it was not long before they were working in perfect harmony.

The little scrum-half and the giant forward may have looked an odd couple, but they earned great respect as a short, sharp pass often sent Taylor charging through. In 1925/26 Taylor scored a then record 36 tries by a forward in a season and Caswell must have sent him in for quite a few.

Caswell could also go on his own when he saw the opportunity and totalled almost a century of tries for Hull. His most prolific season was 1922/23 when he finished sixth in the game's try chart with 24 and Taylor scored five more to be third. Another big season for Caswell was 1920/21, his first full term in rugby league. After an early disappointment of losing 2-0 to Hull Kingston Rovers in the Yorkshire Cup final, Caswell inspired Hull to a 16-14 revenge in the Championship final when he played stand-off with Tommy Milner at scrum-half.

Caswell was appointed captain in the mid-1920s and continued to give great service until his last match in February 1931. He later became trainer-coach to the first team and died tragically, but rather appropriately, at The Boulevard in 1949.

Bob Coverdale

Prop, 1951-57

Season	Apps	Tries	Goals	Pts
1951/52	33	3	0	9
1952/53	40	3	0	9
1953/54	42	3	0	9
1954/55	38	0	0	0
1955/56	39	2	0	6
1956/57	12	1	0	3
TOTAL	204	12	0	36

Debut: v. Wakefield T. (H), 22 September 1951
Finals: Championship 1955/56 (won);
Yorkshire Cup 1953/54 (lost), 1954/55 (lost),
1955/56 (drew, then lost replay)

Solid and dependable summed up Bob Coverdale. With his craggy face and close-cropped hair, he was the ideal prop in the years of many scrums and unlimited tackles. A great scrummager and tireless worker in the loose, he would take the ball up all day, if asked.

Nick-named 'The Mayor of Dunswell', because he lived in the nearby village, he played for Boulevard Athletic and Electricity before becoming a founder member of Hull's mighty pack of the 1950s. He played in all three successive Yorkshire Cup finals in the early part of that decade and figured in an infamous incident during the bloody battle against Halifax in 1955. During the closing stages of the 10-10 drawn final, Coverdale staggered out of a scrum with blood streaming down his face. Then, when the scrum was re-formed, Halifax prop Jack Wilkinson staggered out of the pack with an even worse wound. Both players were ordered to attend a special inquiry, but it proved inconclusive. The incident was out of character, for Coverdale was regarded as a tough but fair player and it was generally believed it was another Hull forward who sought retribution on his behalf.

His solid consistency earned him three appearances for Yorkshire, scoring one try, but his greatest representative honour was as a member of the Great Britain team that won the inaugural World Cup in 1954. Like many other players in that squad, Coverdale only gained selection because several established Test players declared themselves unavailable. Coverdale epitomised the spirit of the squad, which upset the odds after being written off. He played in all four matches, including the defeat of France in the play-off at the Parc Des Princes Stadium, Paris. But his part in the triumph was soon forgotten, as the World Cup remained his only international call.

Coverdale missed only 5 of Hull's 45 matches in their Championship-winning campaign of 1955/56 and appeared in the play-off final defeat of Halifax. But he lost his place to Jim Drake early in the next season and was transferred to Wakefield Trinity for £1,625 in January 1957. He later had several seasons at Hull Kingston Rovers, where his experience proved invaluable as they began to build a team to lift them out of the doldrums, before retiring in 1963.

Mick Crane

Second row/loose forward, 1970-77, 1981-87

Season	Apps	Tries	Goals	Pts
1970/71	17(1)	3	0	9
1971/72	40	13	0	39
1972/73	33(3)	7	1	23
1973/74	14	3	2	13
1974/75	29	12	0	36
1975/76	35(1)	19	0	57
1976/77	37	12	1(1)	37
1977/78	17	3	2(2)	11
1980/81	17(2)	8	3(3)	27
1981/82	41(6)	9	3(3)	30
1982/83	40(15)	5	1(1)	16
1983/84	21(3)	3	1(1)	13
1986/87	18(5)	2	0	8
TOTAL	**359(36)**	**99**	**14(11)**	**319**

Debut: v. Castleford (A), 4 December 1970
Finals: Rugby League Cup 1981/82 (drew, then won replay), 1982/83 (lost); Premiership Trophy 1980/81 (lost, 1 try), 1982/83 (lost); Yorkshire Cup 1982/83 (won), 1983/84 (won, 1 try and 1 drop goal); John Player Trophy 1975/76 (lost, 2 tries), 1981/82 (won)

Mick Crane was as elusive off the field as he was on it. An extremely talented player, he drove coaches wild by frequently going absent and staying away, sometimes for several weeks. Training was a bind and within minutes of turning in an outstanding performance, he would often be seen with a cigarette. Yet, many believed if Crane had given the game total commitment he could have been a loose forward to rank with the best of all-time. However, his only representative appearance was one Test for Great Britain.

A local junior, Crane showed early promise as a centre with Hull before moving to loose forward. He displayed his creative skills superbly to win the White Rose Trophy as the Man of the Match in Hull's Yorkshire Cup final defeat of Castleford in 1983. Crane had two spells with Hull, the first ending in December 1977, when he was transferred to Leeds for a then record fee for the Airlie Birds of over £13,000. Shortly before his departure, he failed to turn up for a match at Wigan. He was in the Leeds team that won the Rugby League Challenge Cup at Wembley in 1978, but a year later disappeared for several weeks and was put on the transfer list at £20,000. He eventually joined Hull Kingston Rovers in November 1979 for £9,000.

The same fee took him back to The Boulevard early in 1981 after doing another disappearing act at Rovers. Hull knew they were taking a gamble and, briefly, it paid off as he twice played at Wembley and appeared as a substitute in the 1982 Challenge Cup final replay defeat of Widnes. He continued to take the game more seriously, and later that year he impressed in his one Test appearance when he appeared against Australia. He also had a big game against the Australians when Hull lost narrowly in a terrific Boulevard battle, taking the Man of the Match award in opposition to the great Ray Price.

It was too good to last, of course, and after missing several training sessions, Hull listed him at £25,000 in February 1983. But he finished the season with 40 appearances, continued the next campaign and then was absent again before returning for one last season in 1986/87.

Lee Crooks

Second row/prop, 1980-87

Season	Apps	Tries	Goals	Pts
1980/81	5(2)	0	0	0
1981/82	42(7)	7	118(3)	254
1982/83	41	11	115(2)	261
1983/84	20(1)	6	36	96
1984/85	33	4	27	70
1985/86	30	9	53(1)	141
1986/87	37(2)	7	51(5)	125
TOTAL	208(12)	44	400(11)	947

Debut: v. Salford (H), 30 November 1980
Finals: Rugby League Cup 1981/82 (drew, then won replay, 1 try and 3 goals), 1982/83 (lost, 1 try and 3 goals), 1984/85 (lost, 2 goals); Premiership Trophy 1981/82 (lost, 1 try, 2 goals and 2 drop goals), 1982/83 (lost, 2 goals); Yorkshire Cup 1982/83 (won, 2 goals and 2 drop goals), 1983/84 (won), 1984/85 (won, 1 try), 1986/87 (lost, 4 goals); John Player Trophy 1981/82 (won, 4 goals), 1984/85 (lost)

From the moment Lee Crooks made his debut for Hull at just over seventeen years of age, it was obvious that he was an exceptional talent. By the time he was twenty he had played a key role in Hull winning the Rugby League Challenge Cup for the first time in sixty-eight years, won a Championship medal and become one of the youngest forwards to play for Great Britain in a Test match against Australia. He became Hull's captain at twenty-one and in 1985 was elected the Young Player of the Year.

A product of the local Ainthorpe Youth Club and captain of the first Great Britain Colts side to tour Australia, the eighteen-year-old Crooks had an impressive first full season at Hull. He was a regular in the second row throughout most of a memorable 1981/82 campaign that included a John Player Trophy final defeat of Hull Kingston Rovers and ended in Rugby League Challenge Cup glory.

Eight minutes after going on as a late substitute in the Cup final against Widnes at Wembley, Crooks slipped a tackle and sent in Dane O'Hara to level the scores at 14-14 and

earn Hull a replay. Crooks could not be left out of the starting line-up after that and he came up with a magnificent performance in the replay at Elland Road, Leeds. It was Crooks who burst through for the late match-clinching try and added the goal to give Hull an 18-9 victory that sent their fans wild.

Crooks had a short temper in his early days and it was almost inevitable that he would be the first Hull player to be sent to the sin bin, only fourteen days after it had been introduced in January 1983. A few months later and, despite Crooks scoring a try and two goals, Hull went down to a shock 14-12 defeat against Featherstone Rovers at Wembley. Two years on, still only twenty-one but now in the front row, Crooks was back at Wembley as captain when Hull went down 28-24 to Wigan in a classic final. He had also led them earlier in the season and scored a try in a 29-12 Yorkshire Cup final defeat of Hull Kingston Rovers at a packed Boothferry Park.

They were sweet days for Crooks and Hull, but it was all to turn sour as the club got into dire financial difficulties and were forced to sell

Lee Crooks on the charge in the 1985 Rugby League Challenge Cup semi-final against Castleford.

him to Leeds for a then world record £150,000 in June 1987. Crooks did not want to go and only relented when told how desperately Hull needed the money. Although other players who have left the club have often been given a hostile reception from a section of fans when they have returned to play for their new club at The Boulevard, Crooks always received a warm reception and remained one of their greatest heroes.

He will go down as one of the greatest forwards to play for the club, developing from a strong-running second row into probably the last and best ball-playing prop. He was also a mighty goal-kicker.

Crooks totalled 19 Test appearances, 13 of them as a Hull player. He also went on three tours of Australasia, including the 1984 trip as a Hull player. The Aussies held great respect for him from the time he made his Test debut

in the 1982 series. He was only nineteen, but tore into them with little regard for their fast-growing reputation as the greatest ever Kangaroos. The fiery teenager went a little too far in the third Test and was sent off for punching. But the Australians loved him and he had three seasons Down Under with Western Suburbs and Balmain.

A reluctant Crooks never settled at Leeds and admitted he wasted his years there before finding a new lease of life at Castleford, who signed him for £150,000 in January 1990. He had several outstanding years at Castleford before a persistent knee injury forced him to retire in 1997 at the age of thirty-three. Brief unsuccessful spells as coach followed at Keighley Cougars and York, where he came out of retirement to help them out of a player crisis and made two substitute appearances in February 2001.

Andy Dannatt

Prop, 1983-93

Season	Apps	Tries	Goals	Pts
1982/83	1(1)	0	0	0
1983/84	17(6)	3	0	12
1984/85	31(14)	3	0	12
1985/86	8(5)	2	0	8
1986/87	28	3	0	12
1987/88	12(3)	1	0	4
1988/89	34	2	0	8
1989/90	31	4	0	16
1990/91	25	4	0	16
1991/92	21	1	0	4
1992/93	25(3)	3	0	12
TOTAL	233(32)	26	0	104

Debut: v. Halifax (H), 16 January 1983
Finals: Premiership Trophy 1988/89 (lost),
1990/91 (won);
Yorkshire Cup 1986/87 (lost);
John Player Trophy 1984/85 (lost)

Andy Dannatt shot to prominence as an eighteen-year-old forward when he was selected for Great Britain's training squad preparing for the 1984 tour of Australian and New Zealand after only seven first-team matches. Although the former Villa Youth Club player failed to gain selection for the tour, it was clear big things were expected of the youngster.

He played 6 times for the Great Britain Under-21 side and was still a teenager when he appeared at prop in his first senior Test match, against France in March 1985. Dannatt was in the second row for the return match two weeks later, but his only other Test appearance came six years later. He also made one substitute appearance for Yorkshire, going on in the 1985 inaugural War of the Roses match against Lancashire.

An early blow for the young Dannatt was being ruled of the 1985 Cup final at Wembley because of a broken thumb, sustained in a Premiership Trophy game a week earlier. Although Dannatt did not quite justify all the great expectations, he remained a formidable prop for several years. At 6ft 2in and over 16st,

his aggressive style caused the opposition plenty of problems and occasionally heaped up trouble for him. He was sent off after only four minutes of the 1986 Yorkshire Cup final defeat by Castleford, and in 1991 he was suspended for eight matches after breaking Ellery Hanley's jaw in an off-the-ball tackle during a Regal Trophy tie against Leeds.

Dannatt's club highlight came with Hull's shock 14-4 defeat of Widnes in the 1991 Premiership Trophy final at Old Trafford. The Airlie Birds had been given little chance against a side who had won the trophy for the three previous years, but Dannatt played a major role in Hull's forward dominance to such an extent that even Hull's backs began to get the better of their more illustrious opponents.

Dannatt gave Hull ten years of solid service to earn a benefit, but at the end of it he could not agree terms and transferred to St Helens for a tribunal fixed fee of £80,000 in September 1993. Two years later he moved to Hull Kingston Rovers, where he achieved his ambition of playing at Wembley, albeit in the little regarded 1997 Silk Cut Plate final. His seventeen-year career came to an end in 1997.

Steve Darmody

Second row/loose forward, 1912-15

Season	Apps	Tries	Goals	Pts
1912/13	35	5	6	27
1913/14	30	5	3	21
1914/15	24	6	6	30
TOTAL	89	16	15	78

Debut: v. York (H), 5 September 1912
Finals: Rugby League Cup 1913/14 (won);
Yorkshire Cup 1912/13 (lost), 1914/15 (lost)

Hull led the way in signing top Australian players after the early Kangaroos tours and one of the best captures they made was Steve Darmody. The 1911/12 tour brochure described the South Sydney player as: 'A brilliant forward who can take his place in the backs. One of whom Australia expects much.'

Australia's great expectations were not to be fulfilled, at least not with his country as the promising nineteen-year-old joined Hull after the tour and soon became a big favourite with The Boulevard crowd. At 5ft 9in and 12st 6lb, Darmody was a fine all-round athlete, as well as a top-class hurdler. Although a skilful player, he was reported as being 'something of a wild man' on the 1911 tour and was one of four players sent off in a violent match at Widnes.

Hull made full use of Darmody's utility in his first season, playing him on the wing for the first few matches and at centre for one game before he settled down at second row or loose forward. Within three months he was playing in his first Cup final, a 17-3 Yorkshire Cup defeat by Batley at Headingley. The following season he shared in Hull's greatest triumph to date when they beat Wakefield Trinity 6-0 in the Rugby League Challenge Cup final at Halifax's Thrum Hall.

Darmody was one of three Australian internationals, along with Bert Gilbert and Jimmy Devereux, who brought a touch of glamour to Hull's 1914 Challenge Cup-winning side. They were idolised by the fans, and all three backed up their star status with top-class performances on the field. A report of Hull's Cup final defeat of Wakefield Trinity sums up Darmody's contribution: 'The Australian found his valuable assistance was needed in the role of a hard-working forward. Right well he played, too. It was the sort of game in which he revelled. Steve would be an ideal three-quarter for Wakefield. And wouldn't they welcome him. He would add that stiffening so much needed in dash and attack. But Darmody is one of the players Hull look to for further Cup successes in the next three years.'

Unfortunately, the next three years would see his career come to an abrupt and tragic end, just as he was at his peak. He had another good season in 1914/15 and then, following the outbreak of the First World War, he volunteered for the Motor Transport Section. It was while serving in Flanders that he was wounded and lost a foot. Remarkably, 'Tracker', as he was known in Australia, then joined the Royal Flying Corps and continued his brave war effort with an artificial leg. Hull later staged a benefit match for him between East Riding and West Riding, which raised over £200.

Chris Davidson

Scrum-half, 1964-78

Season	Apps	Tries	Goals	Pts
1963/64	3	1	0	3
1964/65	5(1)	0	1	2
1965/66	0	0	0	0
1966/67	5(2)	0	0	0
1967/68	39	21	15	93
1968/69	37	10	4	38
1969/70	38	10	1	32
1970/71	26(1)	10	11	52
1971/72	6(2)	2	0	6
1972/73	25(1)	7	0	21
1973/74	32(6)	12	69	174
1974/75	20(1)	7	41(1)	102
1975/76	21(9)	2	7(2)	18
1976/77	20(7)	4	5(5)	17
1977/78	13(5)	0	0	0
1978/79	6(5)	1	0	3
TOTAL	296(40)	87	154(8)	561

Debut: v. Wakefield T. (H), 24 April 1964
Finals: Yorkshire Cup 1967/68 (lost, 1 try and 1
goal), 1969/70 (won);
Player's No. 6 Trophy 1975/76 (lost)

Hull may have had better scrum-halves than Chris Davidson, but none have been harder nor more determined. And few gave greater service than the fiery half back, who was with them through fifteen years of ups and downs.

It was typical of Davidson's battling approach against the odds that his greatest moment came in defeat when he won the White Rose Trophy as the Man of the Match in the 1967 Yorkshire Cup final against Hull Kingston Rovers. Hull were the underdogs, but twenty-year-old Davidson inspired them to a mighty effort, which ended with them going down 8-7. Davidson was fired up from the start and had squeezed in for a try before Rovers had handled the ball. The game became locked at 5-5 midway through the second half when Davidson landed a two-point drop goal to put Hull back in the lead, but it was short-lived as Alan Burwell snatched a late match-winning try for Rovers.

Two years later, Davidson got his deserved winning medal when he helped Hull to win the county trophy for the first time in forty-six years with a 12-9 defeat of Featherstone Rovers. He also made the first of his two appearances for Yorkshire in 1969, scoring a try in a 42-3 defeat of Cumberland. His stand-off partner was Roger Millward, Hull Kingston Rovers' legendary international star and Davidson's rival in many local derby battles.

Davidson might have gained more representative honours but for some badly-timed injuries and several seasons spent in the Second Division with a struggling Hull side. A troublesome knee injury slowed him down in his later seasons and he moved to loose forward.

Davidson's career came to an end just as Hull were beginning to build for the future with a series of big money signings. When Davidson played his last match, as a substitute at home to St Helens on 28 November 1978, Steve Norton was in Hull's pack. How much more successful Davidson would have been if he could have had the great loose forward playing alongside him when he was at his peak.

David Doyle-Davidson
Utility back, 1961-72

Season	Apps	Tries	Goals	Pts
1960/61	7	1	0	3
1961/62	6	0	0	0
1962/63	6	0	0	0
1963/64	13	2	0	6
1964/65	17(2)	3	0	9
1965/66	33(2)	3	0	9
1966/67	36(2)	8	1	26
1967/68	22(2)	1	0	3
1968/69	5	0	0	0
1969/70	12(1)	2	0	6
1970/71	18(1)	4	0	12
1971/72	9(6)	0	0	0
TOTAL	184(25)	24	1	74

Debut: v. Bradford N. (H), 18 February 1961 (1 try)
Finals: Yorkshire Cup 1967/68 (lost)

By his own admission, David Doyle-Davidson was not a great player, but that is only if you judge greatness in players in terms of their attack. In defence, D-D, as he was often known, had few superiors. As coach in the mid-1970s he pulled Hull out of a period of depression by steering them to the Second Division Championship, as well as leading them on a memorable march to the Player's No.6 Trophy final.

Doyle-Davidson was brought up in Watford and eventually moved to Hull via Melton Mowbray and Birmingham. Rugby union was his game then and he sounded just the type to join Old Hymerians, which he did, and helped them to win the Yorkshire Cup. Then came a sudden change of direction as he switched codes and signed for Hull in October 1960, despite having played a trial for Hull Kingston Rovers reserves a week earlier. He had also had trials with Leeds A, but had been training with Hull for some time.

He was aged twenty and weighed a mere 11st, spread sparsely over a 5ft 9in frame. D-D did not grow much bigger, but always played well above his weight. A scrum-half in rugby union, he played in every back position for Hull and never let them down. He might not have been a match-winner, but his persistence could exhaust the opposition and he never let up in defence.

Although not a prolific tryscorer, he touched down on his debut after only twenty-three minutes. First-team opportunities were limited in his first four seasons, but he created a little bit of club history when he became the first substitute to be used by Hull. It came on 5 September 1964 when he replaced injured Terry Devonshire in a Yorkshire Cup-tie at home to Batley.

D-D continued to give solid service whenever called upon and his last match was at Castleford on 12 April 1972. It was when he became coach in May 1974 that Hull benefited most from his man-management skills and his ability to get the best out of players. With limited resources he inspired his Second Division team of battlers to a string of victories over First Division opposition in the Player's No. 6 Trophy, before losing narrowly to Widnes in the 1976 final. However, he quit in December 1977 after the team suffered a bad run of form.

He then had a year as York's coach from July 1979 before departing and devoting his rugby league passion to vociferous match commentaries for Radio Humberside.

Jimmy Devereux

Utility back, 1909-21

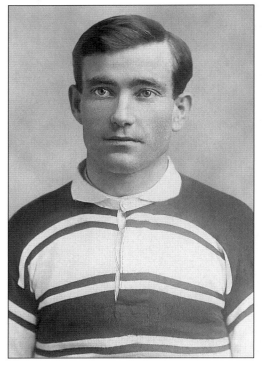

Season	Apps	Tries	Goals	Pts
1908/09	4	1	0	3
1909/10	36	19	1	59
1910/11	22	10	0	30
1911/12	23	14	0	42
1912/13	0	0	0	0
1913/14	24	9	1	29
1914/15	29	21	2	67
1918/19	12	13	0	39
1919/20	7	3	0	9
1920/21	23	12	0	36
TOTAL	180	102	4	314

Debut: v. Keighley (H), 20 March 1909 (1 try)
Finals: Rugby League Cup 1909/10 (drew, then
lost replay), 1913/14 (won);
Championship 1920/21 (won, 1 try);
Yorkshire Cup 1914/15 (lost)

After the Kangaroos' inaugural tour of 1908/09, Jimmy Devereux and Andy Morton were the first of many Australians to be signed by Hull. Although Morton did not stay long, Devereux became their longest-serving overseas players of all-time, and his 102 tries are still the most scored by an Australian for the club.

He was a utility back at The Boulevard for twelve years, and would have made far more than 180 appearances had the First World War not robbed him of three seasons. Injuries also hampered his career and he missed the whole of the 1912/13 campaign when he was granted leave of absence to return to Australia.

Devereux was in at the beginning of international rugby league in Australia and played in their first ever Test match, against New Zealand, on 9 May 1908. A North Sydney player, he was then selected for the Kangaroos pioneering tour and later that year played in Australia's first Test match against Great Britain. The match was a personal triumph for Devereux, as he scored a hat-trick of tries in the 22-22 draw. They helped him to finish as the tourists' top tryscorer with 17 in 30 appearances, mostly at centre.

Even before the end of the tour, several of the Australians were being linked with English clubs and Hull acted quickly to sign Devereux and Morton. Within two weeks of the tourists' last match, they were making their club debut as a centre pair, Devereux marking it with the first of his 102 tries. In later seasons he became more of a utility player and played centre, wing and stand-off in a variety of finals. He was only small and slightly built, but had pace and plenty of skills.

Devereux made three extraordinarily varied representative appearances within twelve months. First he made a guest appearance for the 1910 Great Britain touring side against Newcastle and District, and then played for a Colonials XIII against the returned tourists. The following year, Devereux had the rare distinction for an Australian of playing for Yorkshire, and the match took place at The Boulevard, where he scored two tries in the defeat of Lancashire.

Devereux finished his long Hull career in style, scoring a try in the 16-14 Championship final defeat of Hull Kingston Rovers at Headingley in 1921.

Terry Devonshire
Wing/stand-off, 1960-68, 1970-74

Season	Apps	Tries	Goals	Pts
1959/60	6	4	0	12
1960/61	15	9	0	27
1961/62	3	0	0	0
1962/63	35	13	0	39
1963/64	26	12	0	36
1964/65	24(1)	14	0	42
1965/66	38	17	0	51
1966/67	27(1)	9	0	27
1967/68	27	12	0	36
1970/71	18(4)	5	0	15
1971/72	41(1)	6	0	18
1972/73	32	10	1	32
1973/74	35	11	0	33
1974/75	6(1)	0	0	0
TOTAL	333(8)	122	1	368

Debut: v. Doncaster (A), 16 April 1960 (1 try)
Finals: Yorkshire Cup 1967/68 (lost)

He did not make any representative appearances and played in only one Cup final, but Terry Devonshire was a stalwart for Hull during a turbulent fifteen years for the club. A winger or stand-off, he played in more than 300 matches and scored well over 100 tries.

He can also claim to hold the record for scoring what must be the quickest try by anyone playing his first game of senior rugby league – in just thirty seconds. It was a remarkable beginning for a youngster who had waited two years for his promotion, despite several promising performances for the A team. He had played mostly on the wing or at stand-off for the reserves, but made his first-team debut at scrum-half and showed characteristic support play and pace to go in for his sensational first try at Doncaster on 16 April 1960.

Devonshire's next five senior games were on the wing and his form was such that he suddenly became a contender for Hull's team to face Wakefield Trinity at Wembley. But though he was in the seventeen-man squad, he just missed out. Devonshire was also involved in a bit of club history when he became the first Hull player to be substituted. The substitution rule had just been introduced, but only for injuries and he was replaced by David Doyle-Davidson in a Yorkshire Cup tie, at home to Batley on 5 September 1964.

An outstanding junior with Craven Street on the east side of the city, Devonshire crossed the river to sign for Hull as a teenager in 1958. Despite his quick-scoring debut, it was another two seasons before he became an established first-team player. He became unsettled at his lack of opportunities and asked for a transfer, and was listed at £1,000. However, he asked to come off the list after an outstanding game opposite Castleford Test stand-off Alan Hardisty in August 1962. That began six years of regular first-team games before he became unsettled again and went to York for two seasons. He returned to Hull in September 1970 and resumed being one of their most consistent performers during some depressing years for the club. He played his last game in September 1974.

Gary Divorty

Loose forward, 1983-89, 1995-97

Season	Apps	Tries	Goals	Pts
1983/84	31(5)	5	19(3)	55
1984/85	26(4)	6	1(1)	25
1985/86	30(7)	5	1	22
1986/87	21(11)	4	1(1)	17
1987/88	35(2)	14	5(5)	61
1988/89	33(1)	8	0	32
1995/96	18(1)	3	2(2)	14
1996/97	23	12	0	48
1997/98	15(5)	3	1(1)	13
TOTAL	232(36)	60	30(13)	287

Debut: v. Castleford (A), 28 August 1983
Finals: Rugby League Cup 1984/85 (lost, 1 try);
Premiership Trophy 1988/89 (lost);
Yorkshire Cup 1984/85 (won), 1986/87 (lost);
John Player Trophy 1984/85 (lost)

Few players have made the rapid representative progress that Gary Divorty achieved within two years of signing for Hull. The young loose forward was much in demand after his success with the 1983 BARLA Youth squad's tour of New Zealand and he was quickly snapped up by Hull. Seen as the successor to the great Steve Norton, Divorty had replaced him by the end of the season and was considered unlucky not to have been chosen for Great Britain's 1984 tour squad to Australasia.

The following season went even better as he progressed through the Yorkshire Colts, Great Britain Colts and Great Britain Under-21 sides to make two senior Test appearances against France. There was more glory with Hull at Wembley, albeit in defeat. Divorty came off the substitutes' bench to score one of the three late tries when Hull made a thrilling, but ultimately fruitless attempt to overcome Wigan's 28-12 lead.

However, after Divorty's meteoric early success, his progress slowed down and he never quite fulfilled all of his rich promise. Although

he went on to make six appearances for Great Britain Under-21s, his Test career was already over. Perhaps too much was expected of the 6ft 2in superbly-built blond athlete with Beach Boy good looks. In addition to taking over from Norton, he was likened to another of Hull's legendary loose forwards, Johnny Whiteley. There was also a link with the Drake twins, as he was signed from the same Heworth amateur club in York for whom the two great Hull forwards of the 1950s played.

Putting aside all the things expected of him, Divorty still became a first-class loose forward in the classic mould. Long-striding, with a good turn of speed, he had the handling skills of a centre and was a good cover tackler. Leeds knew all this when they signed him for a tribunal-fixed fee of £120,000 in September 1989. During his two years at Leeds he had a brief spell with Australian club Gold Coast before moving to Halifax in August 1992. Divorty returned to Hull in September 1995 for three more seasons and became captain before finishing his career with Wakefield Trinity in 1997.

Season	Apps	Tries	Goals	Pts
1952/53	2	2	0	6
1953/54	1	1	0	3
1954/55	19	11	0	33
1955/56	34	17	2	55
1956/57	39	19	10	77
1957/58	30	18	0	54
1958/59	38	14	0	42
1959/60	25	6	2	22
1960/61	39	10	26	82
1961/62	34	2	11	28
1962/63	22	1	2	7
1963/64	10	0	0	0
Total	293	101	53	409

Debut: v. Halifax (H), 11 April 1953
Finals: Rugby League Cup 1958/59 (lost);
Championship 1955/56 (won), 1956/57 (lost);
Yorkshire Cup 1955/56 (drew, then lost replay),
1959/60 (lost)

Bill Drake was the taller of the most famous twins to play rugby league. With brother Jim, he became a member of Hull's mighty pack of the 1950s after both began in the backs. Bill's first few senior appearances for Hull were on the wing, and he did not gain a regular place until he was moved into the pack during the 1954/55 season, first at loose forward and later in the second row.

The twins did not appear together until 6 November 1954, when Jim was at prop and Bill at loose forward in a 9-7 home defeat against Hunslet. It was an inauspicious start for a combination that was to play a major role in Hull's forward domination of the next few years.

At 6ft 1in, Bill was more athletic-looking than his thick-set brother. He was also a more gifted player, retaining the pace of his wing days and developing into a second row with subtle ball-handling skills. He could open up the tightest of defences with just a hint of a dummy and put others through gaps with the ability of a centre.

It is a reflection of the number of other first-class second rowers around at the time that Drake did not make his one Test appearance for Great Britain until 1962, and then only after he had slowed down and moved into the front row. He had made his one appearance for England two weeks earlier. At his peak he was selected for a tour trial match in 1958, but failed to gain selection for the trip. Cumberland took greater advantage of his talents and he made 10 appearances for them while on Hull's books. Although signed by Hull from York amateur club Heworth, the Drake twins were born in Workington.

After twelve years at The Boulevard, Bill Drake was granted a transfer request on the night Roy Francis resigned as coach to take over at Leeds in October 1963. Although the two moves were not connected, Drake followed Francis to Leeds a month later for £1,500. He moved on to York in February 1965 and finished his career there two years later.

Jim Drake

Prop, 1951-61

Season	Apps	Tries	Goals	Pts
1950/51	5	0	0	0
1951/52	33	5	0	15
1952/53	2	0	0	0
1953/54	9	1	0	3
1954/55	10	0	0	0
1955/56	10	1	1	5
1956/57	44	12	0	36
1957/58	30	7	0	21
1958/59	20	2	0	6
1959/60	40	6	0	18
1960/61	29	3	0	9
1961/62	11	1	0	3
TOTAL	243	38	1	116

Debut: v. Featherstone R. (H), 26 March 1951
Finals: Rugby League Cup 1958/59 (lost);
Championship 1956/57 (lost); Yorkshire Cup
1959/60 (lost)

The elder of the Drake twins (by ten minutes), Jim made his first-team debut two years ahead of Bill. Signed from York amateur club Heworth, he first made his mark as a lightweight full-back, weighing just over 11st, before moving to loose forward in his second season. He was then struck by rheumatic fever and was out of action for about a year. His weight shot up to 17st, leading to an inevitable move to prop. Although he shed a couple of stones, he was still a tank of a prop and with his aggressive approach became one of the most feared forwards in the game.

His first battle was to regain full fitness after being told he would never play again because of his illness, and he averaged only nine or ten matches over three seasons before becoming a cornerstone of Hull's mighty pack in 1956/57. Even then ill-luck continued to dog him and injury ruled him out of one final at Wembley plus a Championship final. The cruellest blow, however, came in 1958 when his tremendous power play earned Drake selection for Great Britain's Australasian tour, only for him to withdraw with a knee cartilage injury.

Ironically, it was an injury that had caused him to give up his soccer ambitions and concentrate on rugby league. He had just been selected for a Yorkshire Boys Clubs soccer trial, but missed it when he was injured playing for Heworth ARL, after being persuaded to give rugby league a go by his friend, Norman Hockley, who also played for Hull.

Soccer's loss was certainly rugby league's gain as the handling code suited his physical approach, which, on occasions, overstepped the borderline of legality. In an era of juggernaut forwards, Drake mixed it with the best but managed only one Test appearance for Great Britain, against France in 1960, although he did play five matches for Cumberland.

After ten years at Hull he received a well-deserved benefit. However, just before receiving the cheque he signed for Hull Kingston Rovers in November 1961 after requesting a transfer and being listed at £4,000. He also gave Rovers great service before retiring in 1965.

Paul Eastwood
Winger, 1985-94

Season	Apps	Tries	Goals	Pts
1984/85	11(3)	2	1	10
1985/86	27(3)	11	1	46
1986/87	39	19	0	76
1987/88	33	13	0	52
1988/89	28	7	39	106
1989/90	32(1)	22	101	290
1990/91	33	11	101	246
1991/92	32	14	101	258
1992/93	30(1)	11	84	212
1993/94	29	8	68	168
TOTAL	294(8)	118	496	1464

Debut: v. Oldham (A), 3 February 1985
Finals: Premiership Trophy 1988/89 (lost),
1990/91 (won, 1 goal)
Yorkshire Cup 1986/87 (lost)

A former Hullensians rugby union stand-off, Paul Eastwood became the Airlie Birds' second most prolific pointscorer of all-time as a winger, with a total of 1,464 points spread over ten seasons. His 496 goals puts him in eighth place among Hull's top kickers. Add 118 tries, and his place among Hull's elite cannot be denied.

Thirteen appearances for Great Britain also confirm his status, yet he would not readily come to mind as a winger to rank alongside such Hull legends as Billy Stone, Bruce Ryan and Clive Sullivan. This is probably because he was not in the classical mould of that trio, but more of a determined strong-running winger, who was particularly dangerous near the line. He typified that approach in the 1991 Premiership Trophy final at Old Trafford when Hull pulled off a surprise 14-4 victory over Widnes. It was one of his bustling runs that set up a vital try for Russ Walker.

Eastwood's most memorable game, however, was for Great Britain at Wembley in 1990 when his two tries and three goals were a major contribution to a shock 19-12 first Test defeat of Australia. Eastwood also had a key role in another major upset when he kicked six goals in Britain's 33-10 second Test defeat of Australia at Melbourne in 1992.

He had been Britain's top tryscorer with nine on their 1990 tour of New Zealand and Papua New Guinea and was the leading goalscorer (23) and pointscorer (62) on the their Down Under tour two years later.

His Test career total of 39 goals puts him in eighth place of Britain's list of kickers and seven tries boosts his points tally to an eighth-placed 106. Eastwood began his representative career with two appearances for Great Britain Under-21s and also played for Yorkshire against Papua New Guinea.

Although Eastwood was a regular tryscorer from the start, he did not take over kicking duties until his fifth season and then landed over a century of goals in three successive campaigns.

Injury caused him to miss the whole of the 1994/95 season and then he was released by Hull after he criticised the club. It left him free to sign for Hull Kingston Rovers, where he finished his career after two seasons.

Harold Ellerington
Loose forward, 1930-40

Season	Apps	Tries	Goals	Pts
1929/30	5	0	0	0
1930/31	12	2	0	6
1931/32	36	5	1	17
1932/33	30	4	0	12
1933/34	10	0	1	2
1934/35	34	12	0	36
1935/36	36	10	0	30
1936/37	37	11	0	33
1937/38	33	3	0	9
1938/39	32	4	0	12
1939/40	2	0	0	0
TOTAL	267	51	2	158

Debut: v. Featherstone R. (A), 1 March 1930
Finals: Yorkshire Cup 1938/39 (lost, 1 try)

A change of position has often seen a promising player reach his full potential. That was never truer than in the case of Harold Ellerington, who began as a scrum-half and became one of the greatest loose forwards in Hull's history. In fact, after making his first-team debut at scrum-half in 1930, Ellerington played in all the back positions apart from wing before settling down at loose forward over three years later.

'Elmo', as he was popularly known, also became an inspiring captain who led by example. His never-say-die approach was exemplified in the 1938 Yorkshire Cup final against Huddersfield. Although Hull lost 18-10, Ellerington earned a Man of the Match rating for his battling performance. He scored one of their two tries and strove desperately to turn the game around in the later stages.

Ellerington's determination never to give up had paid off two years earlier when he played a leading role in Hull pulling off one of their most famous and dramatic victories. It came in a match against Wigan at The Boulevard when the crowd began drifting away five minutes from time with Hull losing 12-3. Ellerington rallied his men for one last big effort and began it by following up a kick by Jim Courtney to send in Ernie Herbert for a try. Joe Oliver added the goal and straight from the restart Ellerington led the charge that finished with Laurie Barlow touching down in the corner. Oliver's touchline goal gave Hull a 13-12 victory.

Ellerington's greatest season was 1935/36, which ended with a bittersweet reward. His outstanding form earned him selection for Great Britain's tour of Australia and New Zealand, but it also cost him a place in Hull's team for the Championship final against Widnes. In those days the Lions travelled Down Under by boat and when Hull lifted the trophy after a 21-2 victory, Ellerington had already been at sea for three weeks. Having played in 31 of Hull's League matches, he did receive a Championship medal and also one for topping the Yorkshire League.

Ellerington appeared in 11 tour matches, scoring six tries, but never played in a Test for Great Britain, at home or abroad. He played twice for England and once for Yorkshire before war came, and he played his last match for Hull at home to Dewsbury on 9 December 1940. Despite losing a leg in an accident, he later became a director at Hull during their successful 1950s era.

Steve Evans

Utility back, 1982-86

Season	Apps	Tries	Goals	Pts
1981/82	22	14	0	42
1982/83	45	27	2	85
1983/84	35(1)	22	3	94
1984/85	40(1)	24	7	110
1985/86	19(3)	3	4	20
TOTAL	161(5)	90	16	351

Debut: v. Wakefield T. (A), 7 February 1982
Finals: Rugby League Cup 1981/82 (drew, then
won replay), 1982/83 (lost), 1984/85 (lost, 1 try);
Premiership Trophy 1981/82 (lost), 1982/83
(lost); Yorkshire Cup 1982/83 (won, 1 try),
1984/85 (won, 1 try); John Player Trophy
1984/85 (lost)

Steve Evans achieved a unique feat in 1982 when he played in the Rugby League Challenge Cup final at Wembley, despite having been on the beaten side in a preliminary round tie. It happened because a few days after playing for Featherstone Rovers, when they were knocked out by Hull Kingston Rovers, Evans signed for Hull just four days before the cup register closed. He then played in every round, including the final and winning replay. The rules were later altered to prevent it from happening again.

Hull paid a then club record £70,000 for the twenty-three-year-old centre, who was the godson of their coach, Arthur Bunting. The fee was a massive increase on the previous record of £40,000 that they had paid for Trevor Skerrett from Wakefield Trinity two years earlier. Already a Test player, Evans had captained the Great Britain Under-24 side and been elected Young Player of the Year in 1979 when he was chosen for Great Britain's tour of Australia and New Zealand.

Normally a centre or stand-off, six of his seven full Test match appearances were on the wing, including when he scored Great Britain's only try of the 1982 series against Australia.

Tall and upright, he had an easy-going style that disguised a fair turn of speed, which he put to full use in the 1984 Yorkshire Cup final against Hull Kingston Rovers at Hull City's Boothferry Park. Victory was already assured when Evans flashed in with a late interception and sprinted 90 metres for a spectacular try that made it 29-12.

He had five good seasons at Hull, including three Wembley appearances, scoring the first of their four second-half tries against Wigan in the epic 1985 final.

When Hull won the Championship in 1982/83 Evans played in all but one of their 46 League and cup matches. However, when his form began to dip he transferred to Wakefield Trinity in July 1986. He moved quickly on to Bradford Northern in the same term before having a last season with Sheffield Eagles, helping them to promotion in 1988/89 and going on as a substitute when they beat Swinton in the Second Division Premiership Final at Old Trafford.

Vince Farrar

Prop, 1977-80

Season	Apps	Tries	Goals	Pts
1977/78	23	1	0	3
1978/79	37	6	0	18
1979/80	28(4)	2	0	6
1980/81	3(2)	1	0	3
TOTAL	91(6)	10	0	30

Debut: v. Bradford N. (H), 23 November 1977
Finals: Rugby League Cup 1979/80 (lost);
BBC Floodlit Trophy 1979/80 (won)

The signing of Vince Farrar for £10,000 in November 1977 was the first in a recruiting campaign that was to lift Hull out of a period of depression into one of their most glorious eras. They needed an experienced ball-playing pack leader and thirty-year-old Farrar fitted the bill perfectly. He had been a fixture at Featherstone Rovers for twelve years and in 1976/77 had led them to their only major Championship.

Although Farrar could not prevent Hull being relegated at the end of his first term, he led them back the following season after they won all 26 matches in the Second Division, with their new captain playing in all but one of them.

The following season was even better, as Hull continued to strengthen their squad, and he became the first Hull captain to lift a Cup for ten years after they beat Hull Kingston Rovers in the BBC Floodlit Trophy final. Rovers got their revenge at the end of the season with their famous 10-5 victory at Wembley, but Farrar had lost his place in the starting line-up and only played the last eight minutes as a substitute.

A recurring knee injury limited his first-team appearances the following season and after joining the Hull coaching staff, he returned to Featherstone as their senior coach in February 1981, but was sacked after less than two years.

Hull went on to greater things after Farrar left them, but he had helped to lay the foundations for their success with his leadership by hard-working example. His appearance was misleading, for he did not look like a typical prop. A former hooker, he was short, balding and far from athletic, but he shirked nothing and was a master at slipping the ball out of a tackle.

Disappointed at not gaining Test honours during his long Featherstone career, he must have given up hope of achieving his ambition when he joined Hull at the veteran stage. But within a year – and at the age of thirty-one – he was a member of Great Britain's 'Dad's Army' pack that faced Australia in the third Test of 1978, having been brought in as a late replacement for the injured Brian Lockwood. He also made two substitute appearances for Yorkshire during his time at Hull.

Season	Apps	Tries	Goals	Pts
1931/32	25	10	10	50
1932/33	37	15	2	49
1933/34	42	10	1	32
1934/35	41	15	0	45
1935/36	46	13	0	45
1936/37	33	16	0	48
TOTAL	224	79	13	269

Debut: v. York (H), 21 November 1931
Finals: Championship 1935/36 (won)

Hull's reputation for capturing top-class Australians was enhanced when they signed Dicky Fifield after he had shone on the 1929/30 Kangaroos tour. The Western Suburbs player played centre in all four matches of the extended Test series and totalled eight tries in 22 tour matches. Although only 5ft 8in and slightly built, Fifield's quick, darting runs made him a stand-out player and Hull wasted no time in approaching him. However, he went home to become player-coach of country team Junee and it was eighteen months before they could persuade him to return.

Despite an almost five-week sea voyage, he made his debut within two days of his arrival and set up Hull's only try in an 8-5 home defeat against York. He went on to make 224 appearances – a record number by an Australian for Hull. Although essentially a centre, his all-round skills and compact stature meant that he could adapt easily to stand-off, and he played more than 40 matches at half back.

Born Cecil Richard Fifield, he was best known as 'Dicky' to Hull supporters, with whom he soon became a great favourite. Three years earlier Hull had signed Great Britain centre Joe Oliver from Batley, and the pair formed an international partnership that ranked second only to the great Batten-Gilbert combination more than fifteen years previously. In 1936 they played a major role to beat Widnes 21-2 in the Championship final, with Fifield missing only one of their 47 cup and League matches. Perhaps their most devastating performance together was a year earlier when Fifield scored a personal best four tries and Oliver got two plus 10 goals as they helped to crush Keighley 47-8.

During his last season with Hull, Fifield made two representative appearances. He played for a Dominions XIII in France and a Northern Rugby League XIII against Wales.

Fifield averaged 37 matches a season in his six years at Hull before he returned home to Australia, and even then he continued to serve them as a talent scout. It was Fifield who was behind Hull's signing of five Australians soon after the Second World War, including Test hooker George Watt and brilliant winger Bruce Ryan. Fifield had intended retiring when he arrived back in Australia, but he resumed playing with Canterbury-Bankstown before taking over as player-coach of Western Suburbs.

Thirteen years after leaving England, he made a surprise return as manager-coach of Rochdale Hornets in 1950, bringing with him five more Australian players and staying for two years.

Tommy Finn
Scrum-half, 1954-65

Season	Apps	Tries	Goals	Pts
1954/55	22	7	0	21
1955/56	40	10	0	30
1956/57	42	15	0	45
1957/58	41	23	1	71
1958/59	36	19	0	57
1959/60	46	23	0	69
1960/61	31	15	0	45
1961/62	34	8	0	24
1962/63	34	2	0	9
1963/64	31	5	0	15
1964/65	18	4	0	12
TOTAL	375	132	1	398

Debut: v. Dewsbury (A), 4 December 1954
Finals: Rugby League Cup 1958/59 (lost, 1 try),
1959/60 (lost); Championship 1955/56 (won, 1
try), 1956/57 (lost), 1957/58 (won, 1 try);
Yorkshire Cup 1955/56 (drew, then lost replay),
1959/60 (lost)

A former Lancashire Schoolboys player, Tommy Finn made only eight first-team appearances in four years after signing for St Helens. However, he totalled 375 matches in eleven years at Hull following his transfer at the end of a trial period in December 1954 for a bargain £500.

Although never a great scrum-half, he maintained a high level of consistency behind Hull's mighty pack of the 1950s. While Finn had many half-back partners during his long career, he struck up a great understanding with loose forward Johnny Whiteley. The pair became almost inseparable masters of the old scrum-base craft for the best part of ten years and none worked the blind side better.

Finn played in both of Hull's Wembley finals of the period and in all three Championship finals. Of the 133 Cup and League matches Hull played during their three Championship final seasons, Finn missed only 11.

A lean, wiry scrum-half, his persistent support play helped him to well over a hundred career tries and he was always alert to every opportunity presented by the opposition. He showed that to great effect in the 1956 Championship final when he nipped round the blind side of a scrum to intercept a pass and go in at the corner for a vital try in Hull's 10-9 defeat of Halifax at Maine Road, Manchester.

Three years later he scored Hull's only try in the 30-13 thrashing by Wigan at Wembley. Hull fans were able to enjoy many times the only highlight of the Cup final for them, as it featured in BBC-TV *Grandstand*'s opening sequence for several months.

When he was no longer an automatic first-team choice, Finn requested a transfer in December 1960 and he was put on the list at £4,000. Fortunately for Hull there were no takers and he stayed on to win back his place and become a regular again until his last match in February 1965.

In an era of outstanding scrum-halves, dominated by the great Alex Murphy, Finn remains one of the best Hull players never to gain county or international honours.

Ken Foulkes

Scrum-half, 1964-77

Season	Apps	Tries	Goals	Pts
1964/65	19	2	0	6
1965/66	33	1	0	3
1966/67	33(1)	2	1	8
1967/68	2	0	0	0
1968/69	2	1	0	3
1969/70	4	0	0	0
1970/71	21(1)	2	1	8
1971/72	39	5	1	17
1972/73	31(10)	5	0	15
1973/74	13(5)	2	0	6
1974/75	18(2)	2	0	6
1975/76	32(2)	3	0	9
1976/77	4(2)	0	0	0
TOTAL	251(23)	25	3	81

Debut: v. Leigh (H), 10 October 1964 (1 try)
Finals: Player's No. 6 Trophy 1975/76 (lost)

Without players like Ken Foulkes, there would be no Hull FC. He was not a great player in the overall sense. He gained no representative honours and his one medal was a loser's one. But Foulkes was a great club man, who helped pull Hull through some depressing times with his battling spirit on the field and cheerful optimism off it. After thirteen, mostly struggling, years as a player he joined the coaching staff and shared in the glory days of the 1980s. For nearly twenty-two years he made a 100-mile round trip from his Castleford home two or three times a week. But it all came to a bitter end when he was sacked after a brief spell as senior coach in May 1986.

At 5ft 4in and 10st 7lb, Foulkes had to live on his wits as a crafty scrum-half from the moment he began his senior career with Castleford in March 1963. It was at a time when his home town grew half backs in clusters. He and another little teenager, Roger Millward, saw no future at the club while the great Castleford partnership of Alan Hardisty and Keith Hepworth was in place, so Millward went to Hull Kingston Rovers and Foulkes joined Hull. But while Millward went on to win Great Britain honours and a bagful of medals, Foulkes battled on with little tangible reward.

He had his moments, however, and the best came when he played a leading role in Hull's memorable march to the 1976 Player's No.6 Trophy final. Hull were in the Second Division, but they toppled a succession of First Division clubs on the way. Foulkes wriggled over for a vital try in the replay win at Leeds and according to the *Yorkshire Post* 'created a try beyond the dreams of the most creative scrum-half' in the 9-8 defeat of St Helens. He had the cheek to sell three dummies before sending in Nick Trotter. Salford were beaten in the semi-final, with Foulkes getting the better of Test scrum-half Steve Nash, but Reg Bowden and Widnes proved too much for them in the final.

With his playing career coming to an end, Foulkes took more interest in coaching and eventually became assistant to Arthur Bunting. He took over from Bunting when he was sacked in December 1985, but lasted only a few months before he suffered the same fate.

Alf Francis
Winger, 1910-21

Season	Apps	Tries	Goals	Pts
1910/11	37	27	1	83
1911/12	29	16	0	48
1912/13	27	9	0	27
1913/14	38	18	0	54
1914/15	29	16	0	48
1918/19	17	25	0	75
1919/20	39	38	1	116
1920/21	29	17	0	51
TOTAL	245	166	2	502

Debut: v. Batley (H), 1 September 1910
Finals: Rugby League Cup 1913/14 (won, 1 try);
Championship 1919/20 (won);
Yorkshire Cup 1912/13 (lost), 1914/15 (lost),
1920-21 (lost)

One of the greatest wingers to play for Hull was almost lost to the game because of his small stature. Hull Kingston Rovers first noticed the potential of Alf Francis when he played against them for Welsh club Treherbert in 1909, but they decided he was too small. He was a utility back then and scored one of Treherbert's two tries in the 22-10 defeat. Treherbert played only 12 matches that season before folding and Francis headed their tryscoring list with six, but after the Welsh club's demise, a Rovers official recommended him to Hull. The Hull chairman set off for Wales, decided size did not matter and signed the little coal miner for 75 gold sovereigns.

It turned out to be a marvellous stroke of business as Francis went on to become a Great Britain tourist and set tryscoring records for Hull. Although he became one of the outstanding wingers of the decade, Hull initially regarded him as a half-back and of his first 23 matches, 19 were at scrum-half, 3 at centre and the other at stand-off. He did well and scored eight tries, but it was not until he moved to the wing that Francis excelled. He scored a hat-trick in his first match

on the wing. Two matches later he scored four tries and soon followed up with all four touchdowns in a 20-8 defeat of Wigan. The Lancashire club were so impressed that they made a big offer to sign him, but he stayed on to finish his first season with a then club record 27 tries.

One of his most important tries came in the 1914 Rugby League Challenge Cup final, when his last minute score clinched a 6-0 victory over Wakefield Trinity. The same year he toured Australasia with Great Britain, but was restricted to three matches after breaking a collarbone. Earlier he had scored five tries against Ipswich and the injury robbed him of his best chance of playing in a Test. His only full international appearance was for Wales, scoring one try.

In 1918/19 he became the first Hull player to top the try chart with 25, including five in a match. The following season he equalled Hull's match record with six tries against local amateur team BOCM in the cup. His last match for Hull was on 23 April 1921 when he scored a try in a 27-0 home defeat of Halifax in a Championship play-off semi-final, but injury ruled him out of the final. A curious footnote to his career is that he had a brief spell with Sheffield Hornets in 1922/23, when they entered a team in Yorkshire reserve-grade rugby in the first ill-fated attempt to establish the game in the city.

Season	Apps	Tries	Goals	Pts
1949/50	2	0	0	0
1950/51	29	12	0	36
1951/52	36	16	0	48
1952/53	20	9	0	27
1953/54	12	11	0	33
1954/55	22	9	0	27
1955/56	6	3	0	9
TOTAL	127	60	0	180

Debut: v. Keighley (A), 12 November 1949
Finals: Yorkshire Cup 1954/55 (lost)

Although he won Test honours as a player, it was as a coach years ahead of his time that Roy Francis will best be remembered – especially at Hull. It was under Francis's shrewd man-management that Hull became a team to be feared in the 1950s. He brought them out of several years of post-war depression into a wonderful decade, which saw crowds of over 20,000 packing The Boulevard for big games.

Taking over as player-coach in 1951, Francis steered Hull to at least one final in seven successive seasons. True, Hull won only two of their total of nine finals, but these were championships and Francis must take credit for creating a side that could compete with the best, despite lacking the buying power of the big-money clubs. He played to his strengths and that was a mighty pack, supported by a back division that made up for any lack of class with a dedication to Francis's game-plan.

A former Army physical training instructor, Francis put great emphasis on fitness, but he gave the mind just as much thought as body when preparing his players and must have been one of the first coaches to use psychology.

Long before he began revolutionising coaching, however, Francis had a shone as a player with an undeniable touch of individuality. Born in Cardiff's Tiger Bay, Francis was always positive about his dark skin, believing it could make you an instant personality, providing you had the talent to go with it – and he did. He was an outstanding schoolboy rugby union player in Brynmawr, where he had moved with his parson father. He later played for the town's senior XV and once for Abertillery before he switched codes when Wigan signed him as a seventeen-year-old in 1936.

He was unable to establish himself as a first-team player among a wealth of back talent and moved on to Barrow in 1939. A year later the club closed down for three seasons because of the Second World War and Francis was one of several players who guested at other clubs. His was Dewsbury and it was then that he really began to make his mark as a winger. He played rugby union in the army, of course, and was that force's champion sprinter.

When the war was over, Francis returned to Barrow and was unlucky not to be selected for Great Britain's tour of Australia and New Zealand in 1946. Many thought his form merited it and suspected he was left out of the squad because of Australia's colour bar. Just over a year later he became the first non-white player to play for Great Britain when he was selected on the wing to face New Zealand in the third Test.

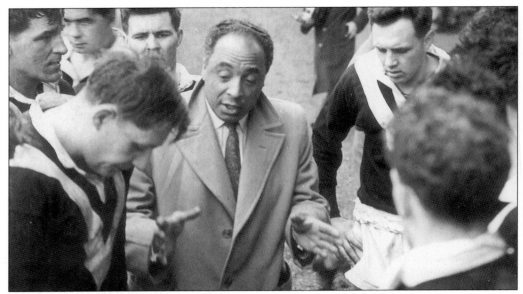

Roy Francis gives the successful half-time pep talk during the 1959 Rugby League Challenge Cup semi-final against Featherstone Rovers at Odsal Stadium, Bradford.

Despite scoring two tries in the 25-9 victory that clinched the series, it was his only Test appearance, but he totalled five matches for Wales.

Warrington, then one of the leading clubs, signed Francis in 1948 and he managed to stand out, even in a three-quarter line that included the legendary Brian Bevan. However, in November 1949 came Francis's most momentous move when he joined Hull for £1,250 – quite a transfer fee for a thirty-year-old in those days. Yet it was to prove one of the best buys Hull ever made, although there must have been real doubts when he was dogged by injuries and managed only two appearances that first season.

Even his debut was cut short when the match at Keighley was abandoned because of a water-logged ground. He partnered brilliant Australian winger Bruce Ryan in his next match, but that was to be their only game together. It was a terrific blow for Hull, who had signed Francis to provide top-class service for Ryan. Francis did not resume playing until the following season and by then the unsettled Australian had gone to Leeds.

Although he was past his peak, Francis still retained much of his class and individual style. His keen anticipation made him an expert at intercepting passes and his dummies could mesmerise the best of defenders. He was also an inspiring captain and during the 1951/52 season Hull appointed him player-coach. He led them to three successive Yorkshire Cup finals, appearing in one, before finishing playing in November 1955. Concentrating on coaching, he moulded Hull into a formidable force with forwards that ran like backs and backs that tackled like forwards.

He was to receive even greater acclaim when he became Leeds' coach in October 1963. The trophy success that had eluded him at Hull was soon rectified as Leeds went on to collect the lot during Francis's reign. No other coach adapted quicker to the new four-tackle rule and Leeds won the trophies in style. He then became the first top English coach to take charge of an Australian Premiership team, North Sydney, in 1969. Two years later he returned to England, and in 1974 took up another coaching job – back at Leeds. Despite winning the Premiership in 1975, Leeds did not retain him and he moved to Bradford Northern before being forced to retire from coaching in April 1977 due to an injured knee.

Dick Gemmell

Centre, 1961-63, 1967-70

Season	Apps	Tries	Goals	Pts
1961/62	34	15	0	45
1962/63	33	8	0	24
1963/64	16	1	0	3
1967/68	16	5	0	15
1968/69	31	5	0	15
1969/70	18(1)	2	0	6
1970/71	2	0	0	0
TOTAL	150(1)	36	0	108

Debut: v. Warrington (H), 19 August 1961
Finals: Yorkshire Cup 1969/70 (won)

Dick Gemmell became only the second Hull centre to play for Great Britain while at the club when he appeared twice against France in 1968/69. The legendary Billy Batten was the first, and that had been forty-seven years earlier. While not comparing Gemmell with Batten, he was certainly a class above what Hull fans had been used to for many years.

A former England amateur international, Gemmell was signed from Warrington amateur club Orford Tannery and it soon became clear that he was a centre in the classic style. His hard, direct running could crack open defences and he would then look to get his winger away. In addition to his two Test appearances, he turned out once for Lancashire to become one of the few Hull players to play for the Red Rose county.

The highlight of his career with Hull was when he led them to their first Yorkshire Cup final victory for forty-six years – a 12-9 defeat of Featherstone Rovers at Headingley in 1969. Gemmell had missed the previous seven matches with an ankle injury, but Hull coach Johnny Whiteley regarded his presence in the final so vital that he decided to take a gamble and play him. He was also made captain in the absence of injured Arthur Keegan. Although Gemmell appeared with an ankle strapped up, he said later that it was his good one because he feared the opposition might be tempted to give a twist to what they thought was the injured limb.

The Yorkshire Cup success had come during Gemmell's second spell at Hull, his first ending when he joined Leeds for a then considerable £8,000 in January 1964. He had a disastrous start at Leeds, breaking a leg on his debut, but recovered to gain his first Great Britain call-up.

Gemmell returned to Hull in December 1967 for £4,000 and continued his good form until playing his last match in December 1970. But he was far from finished with Hull and he returned in October 1975 to join a new board of directors, who revitalised the club and began the recruiting campaign that was to lead to the most successful era in its history. He also became business manager and tour manager on Great Britain's trips Down Under, in 1979 and 1984 respectively.

Bert Gilbert
Centre, 1912-15

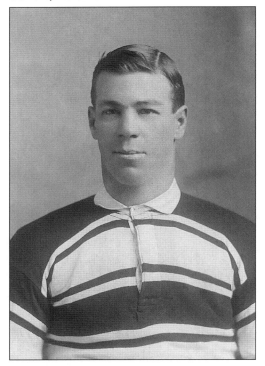

Season	Apps	Tries	Goals	Pts
1912/13	39	16	0	48
1913/14	38	20	1	62
1914/15	37	21	0	63
TOTAL	114	57	1	173

Debut: v. York (H), 5 September 1912
Finals: Rugby League Cup 1913/14 (won);
Yorkshire Cup 1912/13 (lost)

A powerful Australian Test centre with plenty of pace, Bert Gilbert soon made an historic impact as the first Hull captain to lead the club to victory in any final, and in doing so became the first overseas captain to lift the Rugby League Challenge Cup. The momentous occasion was in 1914 with the 6-0 defeat of Wakefield Trinity at Halifax's Thrum Hall. Before then Hull had come away empty-handed from three Rugby League Challenge Cup finals and one Yorkshire Cup final.

Hull's signing of Gilbert was a sensational international coup. He had just finished as the top tryscorer on Australia's 1911/12 tour of Britain with 20 and played in all three Tests as the Kangaroos won the Ashes series for the first time. To capture him, Hull had to pay out a then world record £450. Towards the end of the season Hull smashed the transfer record to sign the legendary Billy Batten from Hunslet for £600. They now had the most powerful centres from both England and Australia at a cost of over £1,000. It is difficult to put that into a modern context, as there is not a cur-

rent international pair to match them. The nearest comparison would be the signing of Neil Fox and Mal Meninga for around £1 million.

Although Batten and Gilbert were together for only two full seasons before the First World War interrupted all playing careers, they made a massive impact. Gilbert had already made a big impression in his first season, missing only 2 of their 41 matches. He shared his debut day with two other future great players appearing in the black and white strip for the first time – fellow Kangaroos tourist Steve Darmody and Jack Harrison, who was to break their tryscoring record and win the Victoria Cross.

Gilbert returned home following the outbreak of war, but he was there to face the first Great Britain squad to tour after peace returned and he captained Australia in two of the three Tests in 1920. Australia won the series and it was to be thirty years before another Australian captain held the Ashes. He made seven Test appearances and also toured New Zealand in 1919.

His Australian clubs were Eastern Suburbs, South Sydney, Western Suburbs, before becoming captain and coach of St George in their first Premiership season of 1921. After retiring as a player, he became a New South Wales selector.

Emlyn Gwynne
Winger, 1921-30

Season	Apps	Tries	Goals	Pts
1921/22	32	7	0	21
1922/23	26	10	0	30
1923/24	33	15	0	45
1924/25	7	0	0	0
1925/26	32	13	0	39
1926/27	43	22	0	66
1927/28	40	14	0	42
1928/29	31	15	0	45
1929/30	40	11	0	33
TOTAL	284	107	0	321

Debut: v. Dewsbury (H), 10 September 1921
Finals: Rugby League Cup 1921/22 (lost),
1922/23 (lost); Yorkshire Cup 1927/28 (lost)

Of the many Welsh rugby union players Hull have enticed to change codes, Emyln Gwynne rates as one of the most successful. The former Mountain Ash and Swansea rugby union recruit was not an immediate success as he tried to find a settled position in the back division, flitting between the three-quarter line and stand-off for the first few seasons.

However, once Hull persevered with him on the wing, Gwynne began to show his true attacking flair and in 1928 he was selected for Great Britain's tour of Australia and New Zealand. The selectors clearly saw the potential of a winger who had managed a modest 14 tries in 40 matches with a struggling Hull side that finished well below mid-table. He justified his selection with a much better scoring average of 7 tries in 11 matches on tour, including one Test appearance against both Australia and New Zealand.

Gwynne joined Hull towards the end of one their most successful eras when a great side was starting to break up, but the legendary Billy Batten was still there, although well past his best. Batten was Gwynne's centre partner in 1923 when the winger scored all three tries for Hull against Hull Kingston Rovers and still finished on the losing side as the Robins won 18-9. Gwynne was equally unlucky in Cup finals, being on the losing side in all three in which he played. For a while during the early 1920s, Hull fielded probably their best ever pair of wingers with Gwynne and Billy Stone, another rugby union convert who toured and played in Tests for Great Britain. They had similar styles with Gwynne possessing plenty of pace and ability to beat a man with sidestep or sudden acceleration. Built more like a half-back than a classic winger, he was just as dangerous darting infield as he was using his speed to curve round players down the wing.

In addition to his three Test appearances for Great Britain, Gwynne made one international appearance for Wales and gained county honours with Glamorgan, and Glamorgan and Monmouthshire. He also played in two tour trials before being selected for the 1928 trip Down Under.

Gwynne's last match for Hull was a 10-5 home victory over St Helens Recreation on 26 April 1930. He later returned to Wales and died at his home in Gowerton, Glamorgan, in November 1962.

Brian Hancock

Stand-off, 1967-80

Season	Apps	Tries	Goals	Pts
1966/67	1	0	0	0
1967/68	21(1)	3	0	9
1968/69	30(1)	2	0	6
1969/70	33(1)	7	2	25
1970/71	44	13	5	49
1971/72	42(1)	10	0	30
1972/73	24(2)	6	0	18
1973/74	31(1)	14	1	44
1974/75	30	6	0	18
1975/76	36(1)	12	10(10)	46
1976/77	34	15	2(2)	47
1977/78	37(1)	7	5(5)	26
1978/79	34	12	1(1)	37
1979/80	11(4)	0	0	0
1980/81	2(2)	0	0	0
TOTAL	**410(15)**	**107**	**26(18)**	**355**

Debut: v. Keighley (H), 8 April 1967
Finals: Rugby League Cup 1979/80 (lost);
Yorkshire Cup 1969/70 (won);
Player's No. 6 Trophy 1975/76 (lost)

Signed from Beverley Rugby Union Club, Brian Hancock soon became a regular at stand-off and went on to make over 400 appearances for Hull. His fourteen-year career covered a period when Hull's fortunes sunk to the depths before beginning to rise to the heights once more. He was the only player to play for Hull on that depressing day when only 983 saw them play Huyton at The Boulevard in 1975 and also when they met Hull Kingston Rovers before 95,000 at Wembley five years later.

Hancock was captain in the mid-1970s when Hull, under a new board of directors, began their bid to recapture former glories. For a time they stuck with bargain buys and local players, whose spirit was epitomised by Hancock. Against all the odds, he led the Second Division outsiders to the Player's No.6 Trophy final at Headingley, where they lost 19-13 to Widnes.

En route to the final, Hull had pulled off a major shock by winning 23-11 at Leeds in a replay highlighted by a magnificent 75-yard try by Hancock, who also popped over three drop goals at crucial stages of the game. The try came after only five minutes and was described in the *Yorkshire Post* as one of the greatest seen at Headingley for many years.

'It began inside the Hull 25,' the report said. 'The ball was whipped out to Hancock from a scrum and he was off the mark in a flash to leave the Leeds half backs floundering. Near halfway he side-stepped Marshall, outran Hynes and the momentum of Atkinson's desperate tackle took him over the line.'

The following season, Hancock led Hull to the Second Division Championship and promotion. After they dropped straight back down again, Hull stepped up their team-building with a series of major signings, but despite losing the captaincy to Vince Farrar, Hancock was a regular at centre in the side that won all 26 Second Division matches to take the title in 1978/79.

Although his only representative honours were three appearances for Yorkshire, Hancock will be remembered as a great team-man and one of Hull's most dedicated players.

Tommy Harris
Hooker, 1950-62

Season	Apps	Tries	Goals	Pts
1949/50	10	0	0	0
1950/51	38	2	0	6
1951/52	39	9	0	27
1952/53	41	5	0	15
1953/54	42	8	0	24
1954/55	36	7	0	21
1955/56	43	6	0	18
1956/57	38	2	0	6
1957/58	35	8	0	24
1958/59	32	2	0	6
1959/60	41	2	2	12
1960/61	30	5	0	15
1961/62	18	0	0	0
TOTAL	443	56	2	172

Debut: v. Bradford N. (A), 21 January 1950
Finals: Rugby League Cup 1958/59 (lost),
1959/60 (lost); Championship 1955/56 (won, 1
try), 1956/57 (lost); Yorkshire Cup 1953/54 (lost),
1954/55 (lost), 1955/56 (drew, then lost replay)

A hooker ahead of his time, that was Tommy Harris. Although winning the ball from the majority of the 30 to 40 or so scrums in the 1950s was the priority for hookers, Harris added a new dimension to the role with his all-round ability in general play. His explosive running, which led to the nickname 'Bomber' Harris, would have made him ideal for the modern game. Over forty years ago, it made him stand out from the rest.

His 25 Test appearances for Great Britain are still a record for a hooker and he is the only one to have won the Lance Todd Trophy. His Man of the Match performance at Wembley in 1960 was one of the bravest ever seen in an Rugby League Challenge Cup final. Although Hull's injury-hit side lost 38-5 and Wakefield Trinity centre Neil Fox scored a Cup final record 20 points, it was Harris who took the top individual award by an overwhelming margin of press votes. Despite taking a persistent hammering from the Wakefield forwards, he continued to make a succession of midfield breaks before being led off with concussion in the sixty-eighth minute. He had also won the scrums 15-10.

It was Harris's compact, muscular body plus a terrific burst of speed that made him such a dangerous attacker. Yet Hull considered him too small when he asked them for a trial in December 1949. They were keener on signing his fellow Welshman Bill Hopkins, a big burly prop, but just one match with Hull A convinced The Boulevard directors to sign the Newbridge rugby union hooker as well. Hopkins was to make only 40 first-team appearances for Hull, while Harris totalled well over 400.

After making his first-team debut, Harris played in nine more matches in 1949/50 before replacing former Australian Test hooker George Watt and becoming an automatic choice for the next twelve years. He was one of the founder members of the mighty Hull pack of the 1950s, the middle man flanked by formidable props Mick Scott and Bob Coverdale, and later Jim Drake. Harris's immediate success in rugby league went against the trend, for few rugby union hookers have switched codes with much success. When Harris made his Test debut on the 1954 tour of Australia and New Zealand, he became

Tommy Harris scores the opening try in Hull's 10-9 Championship final defeat of Halifax at Maine Road, Manchester in 1956.

only the second Welsh-born hooker to play for Great Britain and there has been only one since. Harris toured again in 1958, playing in all three Tests in the Ashes-retaining series against Australia, and he played in the 1957 World Cup. He was also a regular for Wales and played in all seven matches from his debut in 1952 until they withdrew from international competition a year later. Harris also played against a France B side and captained a Welsh XIII against France in 1959. His 25 appearances for Great Britain is easily a record for a Hull player.

At club level he missed only one of the ten finals Hull appeared in during his thirteen years at the club, including a replay. The one he missed was the Championship final victory over Workington Town in 1958 after he had been suspended for flattening Frank Pitchford in the semi-final win at Oldham. A more memorable occasion for Harris was the 1956 Championship final when he burst through for a vital try that helped Hull to a 10-9 victory over Halifax.

His total of 70 tries in club and representative matches was extraordinary for a hooker in an era long before they became just an extra half back. Equally remarkable were his two hat-tricks for

Hull in 1953/54. Little wonder then that the Great Britain management selected him on the wing three times during the 1954 tour when injuries disrupted the squad. He was rewarded for his versatility by being selected for his Test debut against New Zealand. Back in his normal hooking position, he showed the pace of a winger to race in for a try from 30 yards.

Harris's role as a good old-fashioned hooker was never more important than in the 1959 second Test against Australia when he won a scrum near the opposition line and scrum-half Jeff Stevenson back-passed to Hull's Johnny Whiteley, who dived over for a late match-winning try converted by Neil Fox that levelled the series. Harris's international career came to an end the following year when he was dropped after the opening game of the 1960 World Cup.

He continued to give Hull good service until he played his last match for them in January 1962. A few days later he was appointed coach of York, staying in the job for eleven years and later becoming a director of the club until 1987. Remarkably, he came out of retirement to play two matches for York in August 1966 when they were in need of a hooker. He was thirty-nine.

Season	Apps	Tries	Goals	Pts
1912/13	29	17	0	51
1913/14	29	22	1	68
1914/15	43	52	1	158
TOTAL	101	91	2	270

Debut: v. York (H), 5 September 1912
Finals: Rugby League Cup 1913/14 (won, 1 try);
Yorkshire Cup 1914/15 (lost)

Although he is best known as the only professional rugby league player to win the Victoria Cross, Jack Harrison also made a big impact in his tragically shortened playing career with Hull. His greatest feat was scoring a club record 52 tries in 1914/15 – a record which still stands. It almost doubled the previous best of 27 by Alf Francis a few years earlier and has not been seriously threatened since.

Although christened John, he was popularly known as Jack. A tall, graceful winger, he played in all 43 matches of the record-breaking season, which was to be his last as he volunteered for army service in the First World War and was killed in action two years later. He scored in his last three matches for Hull, including a record-equalling six tries against Wakefield Trinity. Harrison had set the record himself against Bradford Northern earlier in the season. Although a few other players equalled the record, it was not broken until Clive Sullivan scored seven against Doncaster in 1968.

Even before he joined the Army and became a Second Lieutenant in the 11th Battalion of the East Yorkshire Regiment, Harrison looked and behaved like an officer and a gentleman. Ironically, in view of his later extreme bravery and self-sacrifice, some regarded his one fault as a player was being a little too timid. The opinion was voiced by a *Hull Daily Mail* reporter even after Harrison had given an outstanding display in the 1914 Rugby League Challenge Cup semi-final defeat of Huddersfield. It read: 'His attack

was altogether different from his defence. Before the beginning of next season I am more than hopeful that the East Hull lad will be found in a more fearless mood.'

The reporter went on to say he made two excellent runs, including one of 75 yards after intercepting and beating half-a-dozen opponents, which was eventually ended by a tackle from Huddersfield's great Australian winger Albert Rosenfeld. Rosenfeld must have been frustrated for most of the match by Harrison, for the reporter wondered why the Huddersfield winger was annoyed with his opposite number.

Whatever it was that annoyed Rosenfeld, the rivalry continued the next season when he finished as the top tryscorer with 56, just four ahead of Harrison's club record 52. Harrison's record-breaking season had begun with an 11-match tryscoring run, which is still the best touchdown sequence by a Hull player. It brought him a total of 18 tries, including three hat-tricks. With Billy Batten as his centre partner, the tries continued to flow as his pace took him flying away from the cover for several spectacular scores. His out-

Jack Harrison's speed repeatedly took the opposition by surprise.

standing form would almost certainly have brought him his only representative honours had not all county and international matches been cancelled because of the war.

Although he was born not far from Hull Kingston Rovers' ground and attended Craven Street School, Harrison opted to sign for their West Hull rivals after a brief spell as an amateur with York, during which time he was also a teacher. His first game for Hull in September 1912 was overshadowed by the debuts of Hull's two Australian signings in the three-quarter line, Bert Gilbert and Steve Darmody. All three made a quiet start, but it was Harrison who took the headlines in the next match, as he scored both of Hull's tries in a 10-8 home defeat of Halifax.

As the season progressed, it was felt that Harrison was not being given the running chances he deserved. However, near the end of the season, Hull made their sensational signing of the all-time great centre Billy Batten. The partnership hit it off immediately, with Batten scoring three tries on his debut and Harrison getting two. The *Hull Daily Mail* reported: 'Batten and Harrison were a delightful combination. The more Harrison receives the ball, the more confi-

dent he gets. They tried the dodge for which Huddersfield is so famous. The centre running round the wing and, on the latter receiving an inside pass, the centre coming back again to take the ball, having drawn the opposition. Batten's early second-half try was a result of this genius.'

The pair could also perform the move in reverse, as they did to perfection in the Rugby League Challenge Cup final a year later. This time, the exchange of passes resulted in Harrison going over for the match-breaking late try that led to Hull beating Wakefield Trinity 6-0 to lift the Cup for the first time.

They were to have only one more season together, apart from a few war-time friendly matches, before Harrison was killed in the Battle of Oppy Wood on 3 May 1917 as he made a single-handed attack on a German machine-gun post. He was just twenty-six. Harrison, who had already won the Military Medal, was awarded the Victoria Cross for this action and though he has no known grave, he is commemorated on the Arras Memorial in France. John Harrison Court on a Beverley Road housing development was named after him and there is a photographic tribute to him in the Hull boardroom.

Karl Harrison

Prop, 1989-91, 1999

Season	Apps	Tries	Goals	Pts
1989/90	31(3)	2	0	8
1990/91	28	4	0	16
1999	27	2	0	8
TOTAL	86(3)	8	0	32

Debut: v. Nottingham C. (A), 27 August 1989
Finals: Premiership Trophy 1990/91 (won)

They do not come much tougher than Karl Harrison – or more fearsome. At a massive 6ft 3in and 17st, with rugged features, he was the archetypal prop. In some ways he was also a throwback to the years of unlimited play-the-balls and countless scrums, as he would willingly take the ball up all day, while his immense strength would have ensured plenty of possession in competitive scrimmaging.

Although he totalled only three seasons in two spells with Hull, he became a firm favourite with their fans because of his high work-rate and dependency when the going got toughest.

After beginning his first-team career as a second row with Bramley in 1983, Harrison moved on to Featherstone Rovers three years later for a then club record £15,000. His progress was noted by several clubs after he moved up to the front row, and Hull signed him for £57,000 in August 1989. Hull coach Brian Smith knew he had got a bargain and described it as 'The sale of the century'.

With Andy Dannatt as the other prop and Lee Jackson at hooker, Harrison completed Hull's most feared front row since the 1950s. The mighty trio laid the foundations for Hull's shock 14-4 defeat of Widnes in the 1991 Premiership Trophy final at Old Trafford.

Harrison and Jackson were also in the Great Britain front row for all three Tests against Australia in the closely fought 1990 series. Harrison had made his Test debut in the memorable 19-12 first Test victory at Wembley and went on to make 13 appearances for Britain, although only three were while he was with Hull.

Harrison's valuation more than doubled in his two years at Hull and when Halifax moved to sign him in August 1991, they had to pay a then club record of £120,000. He continued to be a formidable forward for Great Britain and was flown out as a replacement during the 1992 Down Under tour.

After seven seasons at Halifax, he returned to Hull in 1999 for one last campaign before taking over as coach of Keighley Cougars later that year. He then moved on to Bradford Bulls as assistant coach to Brian Noble.

Mick Harrison

Prop, 1965-74, 1982-83

Season	Apps	Tries	Goals	Pts
1965/66	34	0	0	0
1966/67	36	2	0	6
1967/68	39	2	0	6
1968/69	28	1	0	3
1969/70	40(1)	1	0	3
1970/71	43	3	0	9
1971/72	32	0	0	0
1972/73	24	0	0	0
1973/74	36	6	0	18
1982/83	7(1)	0	0	0
TOTAL	319(2)	15	0	45

Debut: v. Workington T. (A), 21 August 1965
Finals: Yorkshire Cup 1967/68 (lost), 1969/70 (won)

Many props are often referred to as towers of strength, but none fitted the description better than Mick Harrison. He was exactly that in the days when props still had plenty of work to do in the scrums and make the hard yards out of them. Although his close-quarter work could not be fully appreciated from the terraces, opposing forwards always vouched for the tough time he gave them. Yet for all his immense power, he was not a dirty player. He did not have to be. One shattering smother tackle by Harrison was enough to deter any opponent from mixing it with him.

Signed from the local Fish Trades Club, Harrison's first game for Hull was in a pre-season derby match against Hull Kingston Rovers and the eighteen-year-old impressed enough to be retained in the second row for the opening game at Workington. It was not until the next season that he moved up to the front row and then his progress accelerated. Although props are supposed to mature slowly, Harrison made his Great Britain Test debut at twenty against France, after impressing in the Under-24s encounter between the two countries two months earlier. He went on to play seven times for Britain and also made five appearances for Yorkshire as a Hull player.

His club highlight at Hull was being in the side that brought back the Yorkshire Cup for the first time in forty-six years with the defeat of Featherstone Rovers at Headingley in 1969. After being an automatic choice for nine seasons, Harrison left his home town club to join Leeds in August 1974 with Hull receiving a then club record £10,000.

He served Leeds just as loyally and earned more success, including two Challenge Cup-winning appearances at Wembley. After eight magnificent years at Leeds, Harrison returned to Hull in November 1982, primarily to assist with the development of the reserve team, but at thirty-six he returned to the front row to face the full Australian Test side, and held his own in an epic battle that saw Hull give the Kangaroos the toughest game of the 1982 tour before going down 13-7.

Harrison played his last game for Hull in January 1983 to bring the curtain down on a long and successful career.

Ernie Herbert
Stand-off, 1934-42

Season	Apps	Tries	Goals	Pts
1933/34	7	5	1	17
1934/35	38	15	0	45
1935/36	43	19	1	59
1936/37	16	2	0	6
1937/38	15	4	0	12
1938/39	40	13	1	41
1939/40	19	6	0	18
1940/41	18	6	2	22
1941/42	11	6	1	20
1942/43	5	0	0	0
TOTAL	212	76	6	240

Debut: v. Hull K.R. (H), 30 March 1934 (1 try, 1 goal) Finals: Championship 1935/36 (won); Yorkshire Cup 1938/39 (lost)

The key figure in Hull's 1935/36 Championship-winning season was Ernie Herbert. Hull had an outstanding back division playing behind a good, tough pack of forwards and the important link was Herbert. Still in his early twenties, he was rugby-wise beyond his years and a hard man not easily put off his game.

Herbert's natural rugby qualities were probably passed on by his father, who had been a forward with Durham Rugby Union Club. Another son also played stand-off for Wakefield Trinity and the two brothers occasionally faced each other in direct opposition.

Ernie Herbert was born in Wakefield but opted to sign for Hull in 1933 after being spotted playing for Ossett Rugby Union Club. He made an immediate impact on his competitive debut for Hull, scoring a try and a goal in a 22-14 home defeat of Hull Kingston Rovers. The youngster had actually made his first appearance at The Boulevard a week earlier when he played in a friendly match against France, who were on a brief tour after just taking up rugby league.

Two years later Herbert made his debut for England against France before a 25,000 crowd in Paris, scoring a try in the 25-7 victory. He played once more for England, again on the winning side in Paris, and also appeared twice for Yorkshire.

At club level Herbert's greatest moment came in the 1936 Championship final defeat of Widnes. He and scrum-half partner Jim Courtney had been an inspiring combination behind's Hull march to the top of the League and they continued this form in the final, with Widnes well beaten 21-2. It is often referred to as 'Oliver's final' because the Hull captain scored two tries and kicked five goals, but he would not have been so dominant without his half backs' mid-field supremacy.

Although Herbert was a creative half back, his great support play finished off many moves and he totalled 34 tries in his first two full seasons. Injury hampered him over the next couple of years, but he hardly missed a match in 1938/39 and played in the first three of the following season before it was interrupted by the Second World War. He managed to play several matches while on leave, but died shortly after being discharged from the Army.

Tom Herridge

Prop, 1907-21

Season	Apps	Tries	Goals	Pts
1907/08	40	5	0	15
1908/09	36	5	0	15
1909/10	39	4	0	12
1910/11	34	2	0	6
1911/12	39	6	0	18
1912/13	38	6	0	18
1913/14	36	2	1	8
1914/15	41	7	0	21
1918/19	15	3	0	9
1919/20	33	3	0	9
1920/21	23	1	0	3
1921/22	1	0	0	0
TOTAL	375	44	1	134

Debut: v. York (H), 5 September 1907
Finals: Rugby League Cup 1907/08 (lost),
1908/09 (lost), 1909/10 (drew, then lost replay),
1913/14 (won); Yorkshire Cup 1912/13 (lost),
1914/15 (lost)

Look at almost any photograph of the Hull team s from 1907 to 1921 and the imposing, figure of Tom Herridge will leap out at you. He is the big man on the back row with a thick, dark moustache. A strict, grandfatherly-looking man, he appears even then as if he came from a much earlier era and would not have been out of place in a Victorian line-up. But appearances must be deceptive, for Herridge was very much a player of the new era. Hull signed him from York just a year after the Northern Union had taken strides away from its rugby union roots by introducing play-the-ball and becoming a 13-a-side game.

It was to become much faster and more open, but it still needed big, powerful forwards to gain possession and feed the backs. That is why Herridge was such a valuable member of the Hull team during its first successful era. His immense strength in the front row of the pack helped them to win plenty of ball from the scrums and he was equally dominant in the loose. His debut coincided with the first appearance of two other players who were to become Hull 'Greats' – Billy Anderson and Bill Holder. Herridge was also one

of only three players to play in all of Hull's first seven appearances in finals – five in the Rugby League Challenge Cup (including a replay) and two in the Yorkshire Cup. The one victory came with the 6-0 defeat of Wakefield Trinity in the 1914 Challenge Cup final, when Herridge led the forward barrage that gained Hull the upper hand.

The size of the man was captured in a little story about Hull's post-final celebrations when the horses pulling the cart with the team in it struggled to get up a hill outside Halifax, where the final had been played. 'I'll get out and walk,' said Herridge. 'It will take a lot of weight off the horses.' Herridge's statistics of 5ft 11in and 13st 5lb seem modest now, but were impressive back then when there were few six-footers to be found.

Although he gained no international honours, Herridge did play against the 1911 Australian tourists for Midlands and South. He also made six appearances for Yorkshire and in two 1910 tour trial matches. Had the war not robbed him of three years of competitive rugby, he would have amassed well over 400 appearances. Even with that huge slice out of his career, only four forwards have played more matches for Hull.

Season	Apps	Tries	Goals	Pts
1907/08	36	5	0	15
1908/09	35	9	0	27
1909/10	22	2	0	6
1910/11	35	3	0	9
1911/12	34	3	0	9
1912/13	27	2	0	6
1913/14	38	5	1	17
1914/15	38	1	0	3
1918/19	15	0	3	6
1919/20	11	0	0	0
1920/21	2	0	0	0
1921/22	1	0	0	0
TOTAL	**294**	**30**	**4**	**98**

Debut: v. York (H), 5 September 1907
Finals: Rugby League Cup 1907/08 (lost),
1908/09 (lost), 1909/10 (drew, then lost replay),
1913/14 (won); Championship 1919/20 (won);
Yorkshire Cup 1912/13 (lost), 1914/15 (lost)

Few rugby union converts adapted to the 13-a-side game quicker than Bill Holder. Less than six months after making his debut for Hull, the former Gloucester rugby union forward was playing for Great Britain in the third Test against New Zealand in February 1908. Oddly, it was to be the raw recruit's only Test appearance, despite becoming one of the most consistent and experienced forwards in the game. A similar experience awaited former Welsh rugby union international forward Edgar Morgan, who was to play twice for Great Britain within two months of signing for Hull in 1921 and then never again.

Although the Great Britain selectors continued to ignore Holder, he was scarcely out of the Hull pack from the time of his debut until the outbreak of war. He shared in all the triumphs and disappointments of the club's first eight Cup final appearances, right up to winning the Championship in 1920. Holder's first appearance coincided with the debuts of two other Hull 'Greats' – Billy Anderson and Tom Herridge. At the end of his first season, he played in the first of three successive Rugby League Challenge Cup finals, all of which ended in defeat, but he was one of a trio of Hull players who played in all three finals plus a replay and then shared in the joy of the 1914 Cup final success.

A speedy and intelligent forward, Holder preferred to set up tries for others and totalled fewer than 30 in his long career. Yet one of his rare tries sent the Hull crowd wild with delight when it brought the Airlie Birds a last-minute 9-8 victory over the 1908/09 Australian tourists. It remains Hull's only defeat of the Kangaroos.

The *Hull Daily Mail* reported: 'The wonderful try was gained by Holder's dash and speed. It was a magnificent effort on the part of the old Gloucester forward and the spirited fashion in which he dodged his opponents with swerving rapidity was amply rewarded by his ability to place the ball in such a position that Ned Rogers' goal-kick could scarcely have failed.'

Like many others, the war robbed Holder of three years of competitive rugby and he played in only 29 matches in the first four post-war seasons. Fourteen years after leaving Gloucester and rugby union, he played his last match for Hull at home to Dewsbury on 10 September 1921.

Richard Horne

Scrum-half, 1999-present

Season	Apps	Tries	Goals	Pts
1999	18(9)	2	0	8
2000	27(1)	14	12	80
2001	26	10	0	40
TOTAL	71(10)	26	12	128

Debut: v. Leeds (A), 16 April 1999

Selection for the England Under-21s trip to South Africa was the height of Richard Horne's ambitions at the start of the 2001 season, but as it turned out, he was not disappointed to miss the trip because the reason for doing so was that Great Britain wanted him to face Australia in the Ashes series. It was an extraordinary end to a remarkable year for the nineteen-year-old Hull-born half back. Rugby league had been a big part of his life since the age of seven. His love for the game grew at Winifred Holtby School, where former Hull Kingston Rovers winger Ged Dunn was the PE teacher. Horne was fifteen years old when Hull took him under their wing and into their academy side before he signed professional forms at seventeen.

Remarkably, he had already made his first-team debut three months earlier. It was no easy ride for the youngster, as he was pitched in at full-back to face Leeds at Headingley. He was one of three Hull Academy lads making their debuts, along with Richard Fletcher and Craig Poucher. Hull should have had no chance, but they pushed Leeds all the way before going down 22-18, with Horne standing out in a big defensive effort. Horne was retained as a substitute for five matches before being given a couple of matches in his preferred scrum-half position. Hull's plans to bring the teenager along gradually proved difficult as he showed maturity beyond his years and his form demanded a regular first-team place.

The defining moment came with his performance against Wigan Warriors in a Rugby League Challenge Cup tie early in the 2000 season. There was no leaving him out after the seventeen-year-old played a major role in Hull's shock 14-4 victory. His pace in attack had already been noted, but it was the way he raced back to cut off Wigan's Australian Test centre Steve Renouf that really set the crowd talking. Horne alternated between the two half back positions plus a couple of games in the centre for the rest of the season. Wherever he played, he used his variety of skills to great effect, being both creative and a decisive finisher.

Even so, his first international came out of the blue, as the Hull-born youngster suddenly found he was eligible to play for Scotland in the 2000 World Cup. With Hull coach Shaun McRae also in charge of the Scots, Horne's selection became almost automatic and he played in all three matches. However, his representative career took a sudden leap forward the following year when he played as a substitute for Great Britain against France and twice against Australia. A great future seems assured for the youngster.

Colin Hutton
Full-back, 1951-57

Season	Apps	Tries	Goals	Pts
1950/51	9	0	8	16
1951/52	40	7	28	77
1952/53	40	6	32	82
1953/54	43	5	140	295
1954/55	42	1	110	223
1955/56	37	2	133	272
1956/57	44	1	166	335
1957/58	8	1	14	31
TOTAL	263	23	631	1331

Debut: v. Dewsbury (A), 10 March 1951
Finals: Championship 1955/56 (won, 2 goals),
1956/57 (lost, 4 goals);
Yorkshire Cup 1953/54 (lost, 1 goal), 1954/55
(lost, 4 goals), 1955/56 (lost replay)

Mention Colin Hutton to any Hull supporter of the 1950s and they will recall his match-winning goal in the 1956 Championship final against Halifax at Maine Road. Hutton gave Hull great service for seven years and kicked well over 600 goals, but it was that one penalty kick which earned him everlasting fame. It came just two minutes from the end, with Halifax leading 9-8, and was taken from 6 yards in from touch, near the 25-yard line. Hutton banged it over and at the final whistle was carried off shoulder high by jubilant Hull fans.

Just twelve months later, Hutton took another late Championship final kick that would also be long remembered by Hull fans, but this one he missed. It came with only three minutes remaining, and was a much easier shot than a year earlier, but he missed. It is generally forgotten that Hutton had kept Hull in the game with four goals, including a drop goal.

It was also ironic that the kick was Hutton's last of a season in which he had totalled a then club record 166 goals, having set the record with 140 in 1953/54. His total of 335 points in 1956/57 also broke the club record of 298 he had scored three years earlier. A club career total of 631 goals puts him third in Hull's all-time list of kickers, and he is fourth in the points list with 1,331. But Hutton deserves to be remembered for more than

hits and misses. His career began with home town club Widnes, with whom he gained Lancashire county honours and a loser's medal at Wembley in 1950. Then he had a run of poor form and jumped at the chance to join Hull in March 1951. It was a big decision to move away from Widnes, but it proved to be the right one.

Signed initially as a centre, Hutton did not take over as Hull's full-back and regular goal-kicker until 1953. He then became their number one choice for the next five seasons, hardly missing a game. He rarely scored tries as a full-back, but was solid in defence and his vast experience proved a big asset during the years Hull were building a pack that was to dominate the 1950s.

He shared in some of the fulfilled potential of that team before he crossed the city to become Hull Kingston Rovers' coach in November 1957, after being put on Hull's transfer list at £1,500. Hutton began a great revival at Rovers, where he had a long run of success as coach and later as chairman. He was also the Great Britain tour coach when they won the Ashes in 1962 and later had a term as the RFL president.

Lee Jackson
Hooker, 1986-93, 2001-present

Season	Apps	Tries	Goals	Pts
1985/86	2	1	0	4
1986/87	0	0	0	0
1987/88	11(2)	0	0	0
1988/89	30	2	0	8
1989/90	32(1)	6	0	24
1990/91	32(1)	5	0	20
1991/92	36(2)	6	0	24
1992/93	28	6	0	24
2001	24(8)	7	1	30
TOTAL	195(14)	33	1	134

Debut: v. Oldham (A), 16 April 1986 (1 try)
Finals: Premiership Trophy 1988/89 (lost),
1990/91 (won)

A Hull Kingston Rovers supporter as a boy, Lee Jackson soon became a big favourite with Hull fans after signing from local amateur side Villa. He was only seventeen when he made his first-team debut and marked it with a try. After making only one more appearance that season and missing the whole of the next campaign, Jackson began to establish himself as Hull's regular hooker. Then his progress really speeded up.

He had already played for Great Britain Colts and, at twenty-one, was a surprise inclusion in the Great Britain squad to tour New Zealand and Papua New Guinea in 1990. Jackson played in three of the five Tests on tour and was well on the way to becoming a Great Britain regular for the next few years. At 6ft and 12st 7lb, he was much taller than the stereotype for a hooker, but he was certainly in the modern mould with his ability to break quickly from the play-the-balls and penetrate deep into opposition territory.

He played in 17 Test matches for Britain, including 11 as a Hull player, and toured Australia and New Zealand in 1992. His eight appearances for England included one while he was still at Hull, adding to his ranking as second only to the great Tommy Harris among the club's best ever hookers.

Flanked by two mighty props in Karl Harrison and Andy Dannatt, Jackson completed the formidable front row that overpowered Widnes to gain a shock Premiership Trophy victory at Old Trafford in 1991. Although Hull's form began to dip after that triumph, Jackson remained one of their outstanding players and it came as a blow to his many fans when he was transferred to Sheffield Eagles in September 1993, after failing to agree a new contract. The £83,000 fee was decided by a transfer tribunal and was a record pay-out by Sheffield. It was also a world-record fee for a hooker.

In 1994 he was named the Great Britain International Player of the Year, and his high world ranking was acknowledged when he became one of the few British players to be sought by a top Australian club in the modern era. He signed for Newcastle Knights in 1996 and won a Grand Final winners' medal with them before returning to England in 1999 for a two-season stint at Leeds.

Although Hull fans were far from happy at the way he left The Boulevard, they welcomed him back for the 2001 season. His fifteen-year career now made him the Super League player with the longest first-team membership.

Ernie Jenney
Full-back, 1924-31

Season	Apps	Tries	Goals	Pts
1923/24	2	0	0	0
1924/25	19	0	1	2
1925/26	43	0	2	4
1926/27	31	0	0	0
1927/28	49	0	12	24
1928/29	40	0	4	8
1929/30	38	3	11	31
1930/31	26	1	2	7
1931/32	8	2	5	16
TOTAL	256	6	37	92

Debut: v. Bramley (H), 18 April 1924
Finals: Yorkshire Cup 1927/28 (lost)

Hull fielded a full-back worthy of a place among the *100 Greats* in every decade of the twentieth century, and in the 1920s it was Ernie Jenney. Unusually for those times, Jenney was not a regular goal-kicker, and he did not score many tries. But his lack of impressive statistics cannot deny him a place among the elite. Jenney's strength was his consistency and reliability. He also brought some stability to a Hull side that was going through a period of chopping and changing, as the glory days of the Billy Batten era began to fade away.

Hull reached only one Cup final during Jenney's occupancy at No.1, and then he picked up a losers' medal following an 8-2 defeat by Dewsbury in the 1927 Yorkshire Cup. However, that season emphasised Jenney's value to a team that finished 20th in the League table. He played in no fewer than 49 of their 52 cup and League matches, never giving less than 100 per cent.

Signed from local amateur rugby league, the young Jenney had a lot to live up to as he was taking over from Ned Rogers, who had been a fixture at Hull for nearly twenty years. However, once he had settled into the full-back job, Jenney also took a lot of shifting. His steady consistency made him a firm favourite with The Boulevard crowd in some frustrating times for them.

Although Jenney was rarely called upon for goal-kicking duties, he did bang over a few important goals – none more so than the early penalty that earned Hull a 2-2 draw against Hull Kingston Rovers in a fierce 1927 Boxing Day derby battle. Hull could have done with Jenney's coolness under pressure in a scoreless second half, but he had been carried off shortly before the interval with concussion. Jenney could also pop over a timely drop goal when needed, as he did to get Hull off to a good start in another close encounter with Rovers three years later. It was the only goal in an 8-0 victory.

His solid, if unspectacular, performances failed to catch the international selectors' eyes and his only representative honours came with four appearances for Yorkshire. They included a match against the 1929 Australian tourists when he kicked two goals in a 25-12 defeat at Wakefield's Belle Vue ground.

After his long career at full-back with few tries, Jenney played his last game for Hull as a winger and touched down in a 15-12 defeat at Bradford Northern on 19 December 1931. He retained a keen interest in the club and became a director in the 1950s when he was able to share in some well-deserved and long overdue success.

Mark Jones
Prop, 1991-95

Season	Apps	Tries	Goals	Pts
1991/92	28(9)	2	0	8
1992/93	17(4)	1	0	4
1993/94	19(6)	2	0	8
1994/95	4(2)	0	0	0
TOTAL	68(21)	5	0	20

Debut: v. Wigan (Charity Shield at Gateshead), 25 August 1991

A ten-minute substitute appearance for Great Britain qualifies Mark Jones for a place in this book. But the massive Welsh rugby union international forward – he was 6ft 5in and nearly 18st – never fully justified the reported £120,000 five-year contract that Hull produced to entice him from Neath Rugby Union Club in October 1990.

Yet Jones did make a bit of rugby league history on his senior team debut for Hull by becoming the first player to replace another who had entered the newly introduced blood bin. It came in the twenty-seventh minute of the Charity Shield match against Wigan at Gateshead on 25 August 1991 when Jones replaced the wounded Steve McNamara for ten minutes before returning as a normal substitution in the second half.

Jones' first-team debut came ten months after he had switched codes and was delayed by a succession of ankle and thigh injuries, which restricted him to irregular appearances for the reserves. But once in the first team he began to make steady progress as a prop, although it was a major surprise when he was called up for his Great Britain debut against France at Perpignan in February 1991. It came after he had made only 20 first-team appearances, including seven as a substitute, which in terms of matches played remains one of the quickest ever Test call-ups for a former rugby union forward.

The ten minutes towards the finish of the game in France proved to be the beginning and end of his Test career, however, as injuries continued to interrupt his progress. He did make five appearances for Wales while he was with Hull though, to add to his thirteen as a rugby union international. Had Jones stayed free of injuries, he would almost certainly have made a bigger impact, for he was an awkward player to bring down because of his immense size and powerful running action. This was best shown when he scattered England defenders to score an outstanding try at Swansea in 1992.

After being restricted to a handful of matches in 1994/95, Jones asked for a transfer and in July 1995 he moved to Warrington where he had two seasons before returning to rugby union when the 15-a-side code went professional.

Arthur Keegan

Full-back, 1958-71

Season	Apps	Tries	Goals	Pts
1958/59	18	0	64	128
1959/60	10	1	20	43
1960/61	7	0	15	30
1961/62	16	0	22	44
1962/63	39	2	81	168
1963/64	39	4	47	106
1964/65	38	2	16	38
1965/66	40	4	27	66
1966/67	36	4	1	14
1967/68	37	6	4	26
1968/69	35	2	0	6
1969/70	35	3	9	27
1970/71	15(1)	3	12	33
TOTAL	**365(1)**	**31**	**318**	**729**

Debut: v. Leeds (A), 13 December 1958
Finals: Rugby League Cup 1958/59 (lost, 5
goals); Yorkshire Cup 1967/68 (lost)

Hull have never had a more loyal and popular player than Arthur Keegan. For thirteen seasons from 1958/59 he was Hull's number one, both in position and in the hearts of their fans. His main assets were a high level of consistency, dependability and a clamp-like tackle. Add to that the ability to turn defence into attack with a strong run, and you have a full-back of the highest quality. He was also a useful goal-kicker.

Great Britain called him up for Test duty nine times and it should have been more, but he was surprisingly omitted from the 1968 World Cup squad after standing out in the Test series against Australia several months earlier. Keegan was particularly outstanding in the third Test at a frozen and snow-swept Station Road, Swinton. He produced a fearless tackling performance on a bone-hard pitch that restricted Australia to an 11-3 victory, although they repeatedly broke Britain's front line. There was no denying him the home Man of the Match award, but two months later he was replaced by Bev Risman for the match against France and the Leeds full-back retained his place for the World Cup.

Britain flopped in the World Cup and Keegan was recalled for the next two matches against France the following season. The *Yorkshire Post* reported: 'Most people will rejoice in the recall of Keegan at full-back. Not because they do not admire Risman, but because Keegan has never played anything but a good game for Britain and was considered to have been badly done to when he lost his place in last year's upheaval.'

Keegan had toured Australia and New Zealand with the Lions in 1966 and he totalled 127 points from 62 goals and a try in 15 appearances, including two Test matches. He also played twice for England and thirteen times for Yorkshire, whom he captained on several occasions. A bright future was predicted for the young Keegan from the moment he made his debut for Hull, two months after being signed from Dewsbury Celtic amateurs in October 1958. The nineteen-year-old was such a late inclusion for his first senior game that he paid to get into the Headingley ground for the match against Leeds. He was an instant success as Hull romped to a 32-7 victory.

He continued to impress to the extent that he kept out the experienced Peter Bateson. Even though Keegan missed the Rugby League Challenge Cup semi-final victory, he was recalled for the final at Wembley. Wigan raced to a then

Arthur Keegan on the attack against Leeds.

record 30-13 victory, but Keegan had the small consolation of kicking five goals.

National Service then slowed down Keegan's progress and he was not considered for the Wembley final the following year. However, once he had left the Army, Keegan became an automatic choice for the next eight seasons. An indication of the high regard Hull fans had for him is that in each of those seasons he was elected the supporters' club Player of the Year. He was also popular with opposition fans and in 1965/66 won the Yorkshire Federation of Supporters' Clubs' award for the county's 'Fairest and most loyal player'. He was never sent off during his long career and was cautioned only once.

Keegan's career at Hull began just as the great side of the 1950s was breaking up and for many years the team put great dependence on his defence. Yet their one trophy success in the 1960s

was achieved without him when injury cruelly ruled him out of the 1969 Yorkshire Cup final.

Keegan continued to live in Dewsbury throughout his Hull career but eventually grew a little tired of all the travelling. After asking to be released, he played his last game for Hull in April 1971. A few weeks later he became Bramley's reserve-team player-coach and was promoted to the first-team role in May 1973.

Later that year he led the club to their only Cup success when they pulled off a shock win at Widnes in the BBC2 Floodlit Trophy final. However, with few resources to build on, Bramley returned to their struggling role and Keegan was sacked in September 1976. He went to play for Batley, but after only six matches broke his jaw and retired. In 1980 he got a call from Yorkshire to take over as coach for the season, as Johnny Whiteley was unavailable.

Gary Kemble
Full-back, 1981-87

Season	Apps	Tries	Goals	Pts
1981/82	35(1)	12	0	36
1982/83	36(2)	8	1	26
1983/84	29	6	0	24
1984/85	32(2)	10	0	40
1985/86	29	4	0	16
1986/87	34	5	0	20
TOTAL	195(5)	45	1	162

Debut: v. Wakefield T. (H), 30 August 1981
Finals: Rugby League Cup 1981/82 (drew, then won replay, 1 try), 1982/83 (lost), 1984/85 (lost); Premiership Trophy 1981/82 (lost), 1982/83 (lost); Yorkshire Cup 1982/83 (won), 1983/84 (won), 1984/85 (won, 2 tries), 1986/87 (lost); John Player Trophy 1984/85 (lost)

One of many wonderful sights for Hull fans in the club's glory years of the 1980s was Gary Kemble fearlessly collecting a high ball under pressure and turning defence into sudden attack with a flashing breakaway. There may arguably have been better Hull full-backs, but certainly there was none more spectacular.

He was one of the three New Zealand Test players Hull snapped up in a sensational signing coup after the Kiwis' 1980 tour of Britain and France. The others were James Leuluai and Dane O'Hara, with all three more than fulfilling Hull's highest hopes.

Kemble had already made a big impression as something of a young unknown with Hunslet in 1977/78 and he was to make an even greater impact with Hull. The arrival of Kemble and his two fellow countrymen gave the Airlie Birds international class behind a tremendous pack and made them into a great team. At the end of their first season, 1981/82, the Rugby League Challenge Cup was back at The Boulevard for the first time in sixty-eight years.

No one did more to achieve it than Kemble, with a Man of the Match performance in the semi-final and another outstanding game in the memorable final replay victory over Widnes at Elland Road. Kemble scored a try in each, and his semi-final touchdown was rated as one of the best solo efforts of the season. The *Yorkshire Post* reported: 'The Kiwi full-back is built like a wand and was just as magical, with a sleight of hand that had Castleford baffled. They were going in all directions as he went 50 yards in a curving run to the corner.'

Kemble had more bitter memories of the 1985 semi-final replay, if he remembers it at all after being badly concussed by an off-the-ball high tackle. Hull won the replay, but Kemble did not play again until the final. After missing eight matches, Hull took a gamble and played him at Wembley. He was probably not fully fit, as two uncharacteristic mis-tackles let Wigan through for tries that helped them to a 28-24 victory in a classic final.

Another great solo try that epitomised Kemble's style came in the 1984 Yorkshire Cup final at Boothferry Park, when he fielded a drop-out near the centre spot and swept through the Hull Kingston Rovers' ranks on a spectacular run to the corner. Kemble had five marvellous seasons at Hull before returning home to New Zealand where he became a successful coach.

Jim Kennedy
Centre, 1915-26

Season	Apps	Tries	Goals	Pts
1914/15	5	1	3	9
1918/19	17	11	54	141
1919/20	34	15	85	215
1920/21	39	16	108	264
1921/22	39	10	76	182
1922/23	38	7	81	183
1923/24	29	4	55	122
1924/25	20	2	34	74
1925/26	14	2	26	58
1926/27	1	0	1	2
TOTAL	236	68	523	1250

Debut: v. Bramley (A), 9 January 1915 (3 goals)
Finals: Rugby League Cup 1921/22 (lost, 1 try),
1922/23 (lost, 1 try); Championship 1919/20
(won), 1920/21 (won, 2 goals); Yorkshire Cup
1920/21 (lost), 1923/24 (won, 1 try and 2 goals)

After leading Hull to two Championship final victories in a row in the early 1920s, Jim Kennedy's place among the club's greats was assured. He also set club goal-kicking and point-scoring records that have lasted for over eighty years to confirm his ranking. After a long and distinguished playing career, he extended his devotion to the club by becoming a director during Hull's great 1950s era.

Local-born Kennedy kicked three goals on his debut and played his first few matches in the second row until the war kept him out of rugby for three years. He then began a formidable centre partnership with Billy Batten, and the pair played major roles in Hull's double Championship success. In 1920 Batten scored the only try in a 3-2 defeat of Huddersfield, while Kennedy's leadership and a great dribble late in the game were praised in match reports.

The following year Kennedy and Batten were again prominent in the 16-14 Championship final defeat of Hull Kingston Rovers. Although Kennedy failed to convert any of Hull's first-half tries that gave them a 9-4 interval lead, he banged over two goals in the second half to clinch victory after Rovers had stormed back.

The powerful centre pair did all they could to beat Rochdale Hornets in the 1922 Challenge Cup final, when Hull outscored them three tries to two but lost 10-9. Each scored a try, with Kennedy opening the scoring, but his conversion attempt missed. Although Kennedy scored Hull's only try in the following year's final there was no hard-luck story as Leeds were easy 28-3 winners.

Kennedy's most prolific season was 1920/21 when he set club records with 108 goals and 264 points. Both have since been broken, but two match records he set that season still stand. He smashed the points record with 36 from 12 goals and four tries against Keighley and three months later kicked a record 14 goals against Rochdale Hornets. He headed the two scoring charts with his 1920/21 totals and had done the same in the shortened first post-war season of 1918/19 with 54 goals and 135 points.

He ended with a total of 523 goals for Hull to put him seventh in the club's all-time list of kickers and he is sixth in the points list with 1,250. Despite his scoring feats, Kennedy's only representative honour was one appearance for Yorkshire, but he did play in a 1920 tour trial.

Paul King
Utility forward, 1998-present

Season	Apps	Tries	Goals	Pts
1998	1(1)	0	0	0
1999	22(5)	1	0	4
2000	24(15)	1	0	4
2001	26(8)	5	1(1)	21
TOTAL	73(29)	7	1(1)	29

Debut: v. Ellenborough Rangers (H), 1 March 1998

The 2001 season was expected to be just another part of Paul King's learning curve, but the teenager was a Test player by the end of it. Surprise substitute debuts for Yorkshire and England were followed by his call-up to play for Great Britain against France at Argen. The additional surprise for King was that he was selected to start in the second row for the first time since he had made his full debut for Hull nearly three years earlier. All his other starts for Hull had been at prop or hooker. The youngster did not let the positional switch bother him, and he crowned an impressive debut with the final try in Britain's 42-12 victory. His performance was good enough to earn him a place in Britain's squad to face Australia a few weeks later, although he was not called upon to play.

King had been an outstanding prospect from an early age, coming to prominence with Eureka Youth Club and Minehead. He then lost interest and stayed away from the game for two years before joining Hull Academy. Promotion to the first team came rapidly, and he made his debut as an eighteen-year-old substitute in March 1998. It was a gentle baptism as Hull cantered to a comfortable 78-0 Challenge Cup victory over amateurs Ellenborough Rangers, and he did not get another run-out that season. His attitude left a lot to be desired until Shaun McRae joined the club as coach the following year. The straight-talking Aussie gave the youngster what amounted to a 'Buck up or pack up' ultimatum which proved the turning point of his career.

With his mind focused on making a success of his career, King began to fulfil his potential. Opposition teams were soon feeling the full weight of his forward charges, as he became an established member of the first-team squad. Even though McRae retained most of his Australian forwards from the Gateshead Thunder squad when they merged with Hull, King could not be left out. He forced his way into the squad with a succession of impact games as a substitute. Adding a few more subtle handling touches to his power game, the youngster was soon being noted as one for future representative honours.

They still seemed to be a little way off until early in the 2001 season when, despite still being used mainly as a substitute, he forced his way into the Yorkshire squad. Again he came off the bench to make a big enough impression to be given the chance to do a similar job for England. Next came his surprise Great Britain call. King, who signed a new four-year contract in 2001, is carrying on a great Hull tradition, albeit one that had lapsed a little in recent years, of producing local-born international forwards.

Ernie Lawrence
Stand-off, 1938-52

Season	Apps	Tries	Goals	Pts
1938/39	4	1	0	3
1939/40	16	4	0	12
1940/41	1	1	0	3
1941/42	0	0	0	0
1942/43	0	0	0	0
1943/44	0	0	0	0
1944/45	14	0	0	0
1945/46	33	8	2	28
1946/47	42	21	0	63
1947/48	40	7	0	21
1948/49	36	7	0	21
1949/50	31	4	1	14
1950/51	33	2	0	6
1951/52	15	1	0	3
TOTAL	265	56	3	174

Debut: v. Widnes (H), 24 September 1938
Finals: Yorkshire Cup 1946/47 (lost)

Hull were constantly chopping and changing their squad in the early post-war years, as they sought to find a team to recapture their Championship success of the mid-1930s, but one constant figure was Ernie Lawrence, who became the regular choice at stand-off for the first six years of peace. It was well deserved and went some way to making up for his lost war years. After making a promising start in 1938, war service meant that he played only one match in a four-year period.

A product of Blenkin Street School and St Mary's, Lawrence was a studious-looking young man, who did not look cut out for the hurly-burly of rugby league, but his air of calmness had a steadying influence on the team. He was rarely rattled under pressure, despite being slightly built at 5ft 7in and 10st 6lb.

Although Lawrence was generally a creator of tries, he struck a rich scoring seam in 1946/47 when he finished at the top of Hull's try chart with 21. It also placed him seventh in the game's top ten list dominated by wingers. He was irrepressible in the Yorkshire Cup that season, touching down in every round before the final. He started by scoring both tries in the first-round defeat of Featherstone Rovers and finished with a vital try in the semi-final defeat of Hull Kingston Rovers. However, the scoring touch deserted him in the final when Hull went down 10-0 to Wakefield Trinity.

Lawrence was handed the captaincy the following season when he was joined by Australian scrum-half Duncan Jackson, but the high expectations of the partnership were not quite fulfilled. In fact, several scrum-halves came and went during Lawrence's long run at stand-off, with none of them producing the consistency that marked his career. Towards the end of his career, the veteran half back was given a late lease of life as he played behind the emerging young pack that was to be such a force in Hull's success of the 1950s. Both benefited from each other, Lawrence passing on his great experience and receiving in return an idea of what might have been had they been around in his prime.

In an era of outstanding half backs, Lawrence's only representative honours were two appearances for Yorkshire in 1949/50, including a 21-8 defeat of Cumberland at The Boulevard.

Charles Lempriere
Winger, 1895-1901

Season	Apps	Tries	Goals	Pts
1895/96	34	10	0	30
1896/97	27	12	1	38
1897/98	26	3	0	9
1898/99	29	22	0	66
1899/1900	12	5	0	15
1900/01	9	4	0	12
TOTAL	137	56	1	170

Debut: v. Batley (A), 7 September 1895

Formed by a group of former public school-boys in 1865, it was perhaps appropriate that Hull FC's first captain when they joined the breakaway Northern Union thirty years later was the highly educated Charles Cyril Lempriere. The headmaster of Carteret School, Harrogate, he had joined the club two years before the 'great split', having played rugby union occasionally for Oxford University. Before then, his first sporting love had been soccer, playing public school football from an early age and later for Radley College, Abingdon.

But, Hull-born, he joined the local rugby union club after completing his education, and when they joined the Northern Union he stayed with them because he was a firm believer in professional sport. 'Lemp', as he was popularly known, captained Hull FC in their last season before the breakaway when they played at Hall's Field, Holderness Road. He then had the distinction of also being captain in their first Northern Union season, which coincided with the move to The Boulevard in 1895.

Reputed to be a fearless winger, with the ability to beat players with his pace and a dodging style, he finished as the club's top tryscorer in their first Northern Union season. His 10 tries may appear to be a modest sum, but it was out of a total of only 61 scored by Hull in 34 matches. He was also the top tryscorer the following term with 12, and again in Hull's fourth season when his total of 23, including one in a Yorkshire trial match, put him third in the Northern Union try chart. His 22 tries for Hull remained a club record until Alf Francis scored 27 in 1910/11. Lempriere set another club record when he scored five tries in the 86-0 Challenge Cup third round defeat of Elland on 1 April 1899. The record stood until Jack Harrison twice scored six in 1914/15.

The Northern Union did not introduce international matches until after Lempriere had retired, but he gained representative honours with one appearance for Yorkshire against Cheshire at Manningham's Valley Parade. He also played in four trial matches for Yorkshire, scoring two tries.

Lempriere's six seasons with Hull in the Northern Union were at a time when the game was still basically 15-a-side rugby union with just a few rule changes having been made to make it more attractive. Contemporary reports suggest he would have become an even more prolific scoring winger had he been around when it became a 13-a-side game.

James Leuluai

Centre, 1981-88

Season	Apps	Tries	Goals	Pts
1981/82	23(2)	10	0	30
1982/83	34	21	0	63
1983/84	40	23	0	92
1984/85	31(2)	15	0	60
1985/86	28(1)	13	0	52
1987/88	27	3	0	12
TOTAL	183(5)	85	0	309

Debut: v. Castleford (H), 27 September 1981
Finals: Rugby League Cup 1981/82 (won replay),
1982/83 (lost, 1 try), 1984/85 (lost, 2 tries);
Premiership Trophy 1981/82 (lost), 1982/83
(lost); Yorkshire Cup 1982/83 (won), 1983/84
(won), 1984/85 (won); John Player Trophy
1981/82 (won), 1984/85 (lost)

Of all the overseas players Hull have signed, James Leuluai is up there with the best. Already a New Zealand Test centre when he arrived in 1981, Leuluai went on to become one of the greatest in the world. He had plenty of pace; the ability to beat players with ease; and an exciting, dashing style that made him one of the top personalities of the 1980s. With his stockings rolled down and brown legs glistening, he looked every inch a thoroughbred.

Leuluai, Gary Kemble and Dane O'Hara were the three 1980 New Zealand tourists who joined Hull in a sensational signing coup that set the club on the way to its most successful era. All three contributed greatly to Hull's success, with Leuluai scoring several spectacular tries that will be remembered for a long time. Perhaps the greatest and most talked about came in the 1983 Rugby League Challenge Cup semi-final defeat of Castleford at Elland Road, Leeds.

The *Yorkshire Post* called it one of the greatest solo tries of all time and reported: 'There was no way anybody could have stopped Leuluai. The New Zealander slipped past two Castleford play-ers just over the halfway line, went round another and had full-back Coen going the wrong way with a double side-step. Leuluai then had the pace to win the sprint for the line. Not a hand was placed on him until he dived over the line.'

Another Leuluai special was scored in the 1985 final at Wembley. He had already slipped in for one that began Hull's late three tries in twelve minutes fight-back after Wigan had taken a 28-12 lead. Again it was produced out of nothing, as he flashed through from inside his own half to leave Wigan grasping thin air on a 65-yard dash to the line. However, it was not quite enough as Wigan held on for a 28-24 victory. Leuluai also had the consolation of a having scored a try in Hull's shock Wembley defeat by Featherstone Rovers two years earlier.

He was a non-playing substitute when Hull drew 14-14 with Widnes at Wembley in 1982, but was recalled to the starting line-up for the replay and played his part in the memorable 18-9 victory. Leuluai also picked up Yorkshire Cup winners' medals in three successive finals, playing on the wing in the last, and he stood out in Hull's 1982/83 Championship-winning season.

Leuluai's top-class form did not go unnoticed in New Zealand and he was named as their Player of the Year in 1983. He also remained an automatic choice for their national side during his

James Leuluai dives over for a try in the 1983 Rugby League Challenge Cup final against Featherstone Rovers at Wembley.

years at Hull, finishing his career with a total of 29 Test appearances and scoring 14 tries. His penchant for scoring vital tries was carried on in the international arena, and it was Leuluai's late converted touchdown that snatched New Zealand a 24-22 first Test victory against Great Britain at Headingley in 1985. He had started the game at full-back, but reverted to his normal centre position when Hull colleague Kemble went on as a second-half substitute.

O'Hara and Fred Ah Kuoi, who had also joined Hull, were also in the New Zealand squad that season, but Leuluai was the only one of the four not to sign a new contract and he was put on the transfer list at £50,000 in March 1986. His form started to fade and there was little interest in him until Leigh made an approach the following November. They paid only a nominal fee to have him until the end of the season, with an option to sign him on a more permanent basis, but he played only six matches for the Lancashire

club before returning to Hull. Although he played three more matches for the Airlie Birds, the great days were really over and he began to drift away to other clubs. Wakefield Trinity signed him in October 1988 and he played 51 matches for them over two seasons, scoring 12 tries. In 1990/91 he moved on for a seven-match spell with Ryedale-York, scoring two tries before ending his career later that season with 13 matches for Doncaster, where he managed one try.

Only 1,557 saw his last match on English soil, a Doncaster home match against Leigh on 14 April 1991. It was an inglorious end to the career of one of the most popular and brilliant players to play for Hull. At his peak, he lit up The Boulevard with his smooth as silk style that left the opposition streaming in his wake. His nickname was 'Lullaby' because he was always falling asleep, but he was always wide awake for tryscoring opportunities.

Geoff 'Sammy' Lloyd
Second row, 1978-83

Season	Apps	Tries	Goals	Pts
1978/79	37	10	170(1)	369
1979/80	21(3)	1	53	109
1980/81	30(1)	5	79	173
1981/82	32(13)	3	64	137
1982/83	1(1)	0	1	2
TOTAL	121(18)	19	367	790

Debut: v. Bramley (A), 20 August 1978 (1 try and 3 goals) Finals: Rugby League Cup 1979/80 (lost, 1 goal), 1981/82 (drew, 4 goals); Premiership Trophy 1981/82 (lost)

He may not have been Hull's greatest player, but few were more popular than Sammy Lloyd – especially among the younger fans. With his trendy mop of curly black hair and droopy moustache, he gained almost pop star status among the teenagers, who chanted 'Sammy, Sammy, Sammy, Sammy Lloyd'. And he could kick goals.

A strong-running second row, it was his record-breaking feats at Castleford that persuaded Hull to sign him for £12,000 in August 1978. He still holds the Castleford records for most goals (17) and points (43) in a match and most goals in a season (158). Hull saw him as a key figure in their rebuilding plans, which were to take them into a glorious new era.

He did not disappoint them. In his second game, and on his home debut, he equalled the club record of 14 goals in a match that had stood for fifty-seven years. By the end of his first season he had smashed two other Hull records, which still stand at 170 goals and 369 points. He also became only the third Hull player to top the goals chart. His nephew, Matt

Crowther, joined Hull in 2001 and kicked 80 goals.

Lloyd's record-breaking feats played a major role in Hull setting an unbeatable record of winning all 26 of their Division Two matches to lift the title in 1978/79. His goal-kicking also helped take Hull to Wembley the following year. Lloyd's six goals made all the difference in the 18-8 second round defeat of York, a penalty was vital to win 3-0 at Bradford in the next round, and then two mighty penalties helped them to a 10-5 semi-final defeat of Widnes. But all those wonderful achievements were forgotten, and many still remember him most for having a rare off-day with his kicking in the final. He managed only one goal from five attempts and Hull Kingston Rovers scraped home 10-5.

Two years later Hull were back at Wembley and Lloyd was far more successful as he succeeded with his first four shots. But after Hull had fought back from being eight points down to score an equalising try and make it 14-14, Lloyd failed with the angled conversion attempt that would have given them their only Wembley win. He was left out of the side for the replay, which Hull won, and retired at the early age of thirty-one in February 1983.

Although Lloyd was selected for Great Britain's World Cup trip to Australasia in 1977, his only representative honour as a Hull player was one appearance for Yorkshire.

Season	Apps	Tries	Goals	Pts
1989/90	25	6	3(3)	27
1990/91	33	6	3(3)	27
1991/92	37	6	0	24
TOTAL	95	18	6(6)	78

Debut: v. Wakefield T. (A), 29 October 1989
Finals: Premiership Trophy 1990/91 (won)

The only Hull player to win the Harry Sunderland Trophy as Man of the Match in the end of season play-off final, Greg Mackey made a major impact in just three seasons with the Airlie Birds. He was also the captain when Hull pulled off the shock defeat of Widnes in the Premiership Trophy final at Old Trafford in 1991. It was the only time Hull won the trophy, following four final defeats, and the Australian stand-off's shrewd leadership proved to be the key factor. He had a hand in two of their three tries, set up a series of other attacks and pinned back Widnes with his tactical kicking.

Mackey had also produced the towering kick in the semi-final, which Gary Nolan pounced on to touch down after Leeds' former New Zealand rugby union international full-back John Gallagher mis-fielded under the posts.

Hull's signing of Mackey in October 1989 was shrouded in controversy. A former Canterbury Bankstown and Illawarra half back, he had arrived unsung at Warrington a few months earlier. Warrington had seen him as only a short-term signing, but he was an immediate success and within a few weeks had inspired them to a Lancashire Cup final victory.

He had just agreed a new two-year contract when Hull stepped in and signed him. Warrington accused Hull of an illegal approach, but eventually accepted his departure and received a small compensation fee to cover the few weeks remaining of his contract. It was one of the best deals Hull had done for many years, although they had to release injured David Liddiard to make way for Mackey on their overseas quota.

With coach Brian Smith mapping out the game-plan and Mackey dictating matters on the field, Hull began their revival that was to lead to the Premiership Trophy within two years. One of his greatest assets was maintaining a high level of consistency. After making his debut for Hull, Mackey missed the next match but was then an ever present in either half back position until he returned to Warrington in 1992 – a run of 94 successive matches. Mackey then played in 98 successive matches for Warrington before being out for several weeks. He ended his English career in 1996.

Alf Macklin

Winger, 1968-79

Season	Apps	Tries	Goals	Pts
1968/69	24(4)	7	0	21
1969/70	21(4)	5	0	15
1970/71	36	16	2	52
1971/72	25(1)	9	2	31
1972/73	33(1)	12	0	36
1973/74	26	7	15	51
1974/75	33	12	5	46
1975/76	32(2)	18	0	54
1976/77	37	17	8	67
1977/78	37	10	0	30
1978/79	23(3)	9	0	27
1979/80	1(1)	0	0	0
TOTAL	328(16)	122	32	430

Debut: v. Salford (A), 16 August 1968
Finals: Yorkshire Cup 1969/70 (won);
Player's No. 6 Trophy 1975/76 (lost)

You will not find Alf Macklin in any list of record-breakers and he never gained representative honours, but he became something of a folk hero to Hull fans in the 1970s. They called him 'Super Alf'. He was one of them, a local lad who got stuck in and made up for any lack of skills with sheer determination. He was far from your classic winger, with a rugged – almost ragged – appearance, but he was one you could depend upon. And Hull did, in well over 300 matches, spanning some of the most depressing times in the club's history.

You had to know him to appreciate him, and former Hull coach Arthur Bunting acknowledged this after taking over at The Boulevard during Macklin's last couple of years. Bunting admitted he had not rated Macklin very highly until he started studying videos of Hull's matches and noted how few mistakes he made. 'He was so reliable,' Bunting summed up.

Macklin's brother, Jim, was already in Hull's pack when Alf signed for Hull. He actually made his senior debut as a centre to the great Clive Sullivan, but by the end of the season he was beginning to make his own little mark on the wing. The following season, he and Sullivan were the wingers when Hull beat Featherstone Rovers in the Yorkshire Cup final at Headingley. They continued to be Hull's wingers for a few more years and the contrast could not have been greater – Sullivan, the sleek thoroughbred, and Macklin, the willing workhorse.

One of Macklin's most memorable games was crowned by two tries in the last five minutes of a stunning 23-11 Player's No.6 second round replay win at Leeds. He was playing opposite Great Britain winger John Atkinson, but that was Macklin's night. He also scored a vital try in the 9-8 defeat of St Helens in the next round as Hull marched on to the final.

Towards the end of the decade, Hull had begun their recruiting campaign of major stars and Macklin's days were numbered. He figured in Hull's promotion season of 1978/79, before making his last appearance as a substitute in the opening match of the following term, but he remained a popular sportsman around Hull as a top-class darts player.

John Maloney
Centre, 1965-71, 1972-73

Season	Apps	Tries	Goals	Pts
1965/66	31	7	84	189
1966/67	39	7	123	267
1967/68	38	5	120	255
1968/69	37	8	110	244
1969/70	37	4	103	218
1970/71	21	3	59	127
1971/72	4(1)	2	17	40
1972/73	12	1	31	65
1973/74	6	1	27	57
TOTAL	225(1)	38	674	1462

Debut: v. Workington T. (H), 2 October 1965 (4 goals) Finals: Yorkshire Cup 1967/68 (lost, 1 goal), 1969/70 (won, 2 goals)

Even in these days of highly-paid Super League stars with flash cars, the sight of any player turning up on match day in a Rolls Royce would turn a few heads, but that is how John Maloney used to arrive at The Boulevard over thirty years ago. It was not his match wages that allowed him to put on the style, of course. It was the fact that he was the managing director of an engineering company.

Maloney also had a touch of class on the field as a goal-kicking centre who finished his Hull career with 674 goals and 1,462 points. Only Joe Oliver scored more goals and points for the Airlie Birds. An outstanding amateur with top Dewsbury club Shaw Cross, Maloney signed for Hull in 1965 and, after only a few matches with the reserves, made his first-team debut, kicking the first four of his big career total of goals. It also began a remarkable run for a newcomer of 92 successive appearances before he was dropped to make way for the return of Dick Gemmell from Leeds.

But the youngster was soon playing alongside the experienced Gemmell and they were together when Hull won the Yorkshire Cup in 1969, with Maloney's two goals proving vital in the 12-9 defeat of Featherstone Rovers. Although Maloney was a consistent club player and rarely gave a bad performance, he did not fulfil all that was expected of him.

Within three weeks of making his first-team debut, Maloney was playing for Great Britain Under-24s against France, but that remained his only representative appearance as a professional.

After nine seasons of making two or three weekly trips over to Hull from his Dewsbury home for training and matches, Maloney moved to York in October 1971, which he found a little more convenient. However, a year later he was back at Hull for another couple of seasons, although his first-team appearances were restricted. He then moved on for a brief spell at Dewsbury and a few seasons at Rochdale Hornets, where he ended his long playing career in September 1978.

His son, Francis, followed him as a senior professional with several clubs and gained international honours with England that evaded his father.

Harry Markham
Second row, 1951-57

Season	Apps	Tries	Goals	Pts
1951/52	15	0	0	0
1952/53	39	10	0	30
1953/54	28	9	0	27
1954/55	41	6	0	18
1955/56	36	10	0	30
1956/57	23	4	0	12
TOTAL	182	39	0	117

Debut: v. Doncaster (H), 20 October 1951
Finals: Championship 1955/56 (won);
Yorkshire Cup 1953/54 (lost), 1954/55 (lost, 1
try), 1955/56 (drew, then lost replay)

A serious back injury brought a premature end to Harry Markham's career, just when he was being talked about as one of the best second-row forwards ever to play for Hull. A big raw-boned fish docker, he was a fearsome sight in full stride and would rather go through a player than round him. He used that approach to devastating effect in the city's first floodlit derby game at Hull City's Boothferry Park in 1953. Hull Kingston Rovers had no answer to Markham's long-distance charges down the wing that night, and his two tries were vital scores in Hull's 15-4 victory.

Markham was in at the beginning when Hull began to build the mighty pack that was to have a feared reputation throughout the 1950s. When he played for Yorkshire against the 1955 New Zealand tourists, also in the pack were three Hull-born colleagues – Mick Scott, Bob Coverdale and Johnny Whiteley. All four were a major force in the Hull side that won the Championship with a 10-9 defeat of Halifax in the play-off final the fol-

lowing year. Halifax also had a fiery pack and their clashes with Hull gained some infamy with Markham always in the thick of it, scoring a try in the 1954 Yorkshire Cup final defeat.

Markham was at the peak of his form midway through the 1956/57 season and having an outstanding game at Dewsbury, scoring a try and causing his usual havoc, when he received a leg injury that caused no immediate concern. However, it turned out to have caused serious damage to his nervous system at the bottom of his spine and the game in January 1957 proved to be his last. He was only twenty-eight. After a long spell in hospital, Markham worked hard to regain fitness and was down to play in a pre-season trial match eighteen months later, but he pulled out of the game and decided to retire.

It was a sad end to a career that would otherwise have held more than his few representative appearances, which consisted of two appearances for Yorkshire, one for England and another for a Rest of the League side in a Test trial against a Great Britain XIII.

George Matthews
Stand-off, 1958-63

Season	Apps	Tries	Goals	Pts
1958/59	28	23	0	69
1959/60	25	15	0	45
1960/61	31	9	0	27
1961/62	28	11	0	33
1962/63	26	5	0	15
TOTAL	138	63	0	189

Debut: v. Bramley (H), 27 September 1958 (2 tries) Finals: Rugby League Cup 1958/59 (lost); Yorkshire Cup 1959/60 (lost)

Few players have made a bigger impact playing their first game in Hull colours than George Matthews, even if it was only an A-team match. The nineteen-year-old stand-off from Barrow junior club St Mary's had a lot to live up to. As captain of the England Under-19s, and chased by several major clubs, Matthews was given a big build-up by the *Hull Daily Mail* and over 5,000 attended his reserve-team debut in April 1958. He fully justified the great expectations and the *Mail* reported: 'Hull A's victory over Huddersfield was inspired by the undoubted genius of a lad playing his first game of professional football. He was in scintillating form, revealing speed and all the capabilities of a born rugby player. He scored two first-class tries and generally showed the form that must book him a first-team place early next season.'

If Matthews never reached the heights predicted after that extraordinary performance, gaining no representative honours as a professional, he was still a very useful acquisition for Hull. He scored two tries on his first-team debut early the next season and finished it as their top scorer with 23. In one scoring burst towards the end of the season, he totalled 12 tries in a seven-match scoring sequence. It included all three of Hull's tries in the 15-5 Rugby League Challenge Cup semi-final defeat of Featherstone Rovers that swept Hull to their first Wembley appearance. Playing behind Hull's mighty pack, Matthews's terrific support play brought him the first two tries before completing his hat-trick

with a solo effort from a scrum.

That was the only time Matthews repeated his memorable A-team debut performance. He had a quiet game in the final, when Wigan romped to a 30-13 victory, and with Hull's famous pack beginning to break up, the youngster found it much tougher going the next season. However, he stuck at it and became a regular for the next three years, showing his versatility by playing in all the back positions apart from scrum-half.

Occasionally he would reveal flashes of his undoubted all-round skills, dummying and sidestepping through the tightest of defences or backing up and finishing off the breaks of others. It all made him look a natural rugby league player, but wherever his talent rugby sprung from it could not have been from his father, who had played soccer for Barrow.

Matthews played his last match for Hull in the centre at home to Oldham on 27 May 1963. Just before the opening of the following season, he expressed a wish to return home to Barrow, who signed him for about £1,000.

Alan McGlone

Hooker, 1963-74

Season	Apps	Tries	Goals	Pts
1963/64	24	0	0	0
1964/65	31	4	0	12
1965/66	35	4	0	12
1966/67	30	1	0	3
1967/68	37	1	2	7
1968/69	3	0	0	0
1969/70	34	4	1	14
1970/71	44(2)	6	10	38
1971/72	4	0	1	2
1972/73	9(2)	0	2	4
1973/74	15	3	5	19
1974/75	2	0	0	0
TOTAL	268(4)	23	21	111

Debut: v. Castleford (A), 16 November 1963
Finals: Yorkshire Cup 1967/68 (lost),
1969/70 (won)

There must have been some good hookers around in the 1960s and beyond for Alan McGlone not to have gained any representative honours. For more than a decade he held his own with the best, winning more than a fair share of the scrums when they were still competitive and making his presence felt in the loose.

A local amateur with New Trinity and East Hull juniors, he signed for Hull after an impressive reserve-team trial in which he won the scrums 28-10. Hull had been looking for a successor to the great Tommy Harris, who had left two years earlier, and after a succession of hookers failed to fit the bill, it looked as if twenty-year-old McGlone was their man.

Within a month he was making his first-team debut against Castleford's international hooker Johnny Ward and, despite Hull being well beaten, McGlone confirmed his promise. He kept his place to start a long run as Hull's hooker through a mixture of good and bad times for the club. The good came with Hull's 1969 Yorkshire Cup final of defeat of Featherstone Rovers. McGlone monopolised scrum possession to give Hull a big advantage, while giving a totally committed performance in general play. He had also given his usual battling display when Hull lost to Hull Kingston Rovers in the county final two years earlier.

Always a fiery character, McGlone was at his best when the going got toughest and was the central figure in quite a few skirmishes in local derby clashes with Rovers. At 5ft 11in and over 14st, he was pretty hefty for a No. 9 but still very mobile and adept at making breaks from the play-the-ball, long before they became the trend for hookers playing more like half backs.

Although injury restricted McGlone to only three appearances in 1968/69, he bounced back the following season and in 1970/71 missed only two of Hull's packed programme of 46 matches. But injuries returned to interfere with his remaining years at the club and he played his last match away to Bramley on 28 September 1974. It was a sad note on which to end his long career, as Hull suffered an unexpected 15-6 defeat in a Player's No. 6 Trophy tie.

Steve McNamara

Second row/loose forward, 1989-96

Season	Apps	Tries	Goals	Pts
1989/90	7(1)	2	0	8
1990/91	19(8)	4	0	16
1991/92	29	0	2	4
1992/93	25	5	0	20
1993/94	25(4)	2	6(4)	16
1994/95	32	2	12	32
1995/96	22	10	101(1)	241
1996	3	1	14	32
TOTAL	162(13)	26	135(5)	369

Debut: v. Bradford N. (A), 3 September 1989 (1 try)

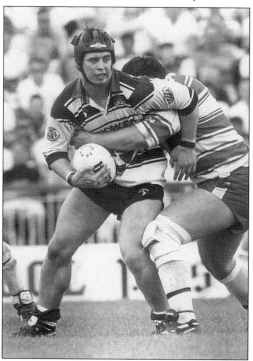

The son of a former Hull and Hull Kingston Rovers full-back, Steve McNamara was snapped up by the Airlie Birds as one of the most promising young forwards in the district. A former England Schoolboys captain, he continued his progress at Bransholme Youth Club and Skirlaugh before Hull moved quickly to sign him in June 1989.

He made his first-team debut a few months later, but spent most of that season in the reserve team, ending it with a Man of the Match performance in the Alliance Cup final. The first of five appearances for Great Britain Under-21s, whom he also captained, followed the next season as his skills as a ball-playing back-row forward began to attract greater attention.

Although he missed Hull's Premiership final victory in 1991, he made a bit of rugby league history in the Charity Shield match against Wigan at Gateshead the start of the following season. The RFL had decided to follow the Australians' example by introducing the blood bin and McNamara became the first to occupy it when he was wounded in the twenty-seventh minute and replaced for ten minutes by Mark Jones.

By the end of the 1991/92 season, the twenty-year-old McNamara had made his mark in more substantial ways, making his Great Britain debut as a substitute in the 36-0 defeat of France at The Boulevard. Hull had just switched him to stand-off for a few matches, and his versatility brought

further reward when he was flown out as a replacement three weeks into Great Britain's 1992 tour of Australia and New Zealand. The call to join the tour came as a complete surprise to McNamara, who was on holiday in Greece at the time. He made four appearances on tour, scoring one try, and came back all the better for the experience. McNamara made one other appearance for Great Britain while at Hull, again as a substitute against France, and he also played twice for England. His value to Hull was growing, more so when he took over goal-kicking duties in 1995/96 and finished the season with a century.

He was now Hull's captain, but the arrival of Super League in 1996 and the club's failure to be included among the elite unsettled the ambitious McNamara and he asked for a transfer. Reluctantly, Hull agreed and he was transferred to Bradford Bulls for £100,000 in April 1996. Some Hull fans never forgave him, but it was undoubtedly a good move for him as he shared in Bradford's success of the next few years before moving on to Wakefield Trinity Wildcats and then Huddersfield Giants.

Freddie Miller
Full-back, 1933-49

Season	Apps	Tries	Goals	Pts
1932/33	1	0	3	6
1933/34	30	3	21	43
1934/35	46	3	24	57
1935/36	47	0	39	78
1936/37	40	2	22	50
1937/38	38	3	31	71
1938/39	44	3	101	211
1939/40	27	3	59	127
1940/41	6	1	15	33
1941/42	2	0	5	10
1942/43	2	0	4	8
1943/44	0	0	0	0
1944/45	0	0	0	0
1945/46	16	0	28	56
1946/47	42	3	103	215
1947/48	39	2	89	184
1948/49	4	0	7	14
1949/50	1	0	7	14
TOTAL	385	23	558	1185

Debut: v. Dewsbury (A), 18 April 1933 (3 goals)
Finals: Championship 1935/36 (won, 1 goal);
Yorkshire Cup 1938/39 (lost, 2 goals),
1946/47 (lost)

In the years when kicking duels between full-backs in general play were a feature of the game, Freddie Miller rarely came off second best. His mighty boot would often send the ball way beyond his opponent and he regularly found touch from over 50 yards. He was also a prodigious goal-kicker and though the Second World War limited him to less than a dozen games over five years, he still finished high up in Hull's career goals chart with 558. They included many drop goals, another skill in which he had no superior.

Although not even his most ardent admirers would compare Miller favourably with Jim Sullivan, he was similar in build and style as the legendary Wigan and Great Britain full-back. Both were big, sturdy full-backs, who were solid in defence and decisive in attack. They clashed half-a-dozen times in the 1930s when the young Miller was just emerging as an outstanding talent and Sullivan had many years of Test experience behind him.

Veteran Hull fans always claim Sullivan could never out-kick Miller. There were other top-class full-backs around then, including Jim Brough

and Yorkshire's Jack Walkington, which limited Miller's representative appearances. Even as late as 1947, New Zealand full-back Warwick Clarke rated Miller the best full-back he had faced on that year's Kiwis tour.

The nearest he came to international honours was when he played in a 1936 tour trial and failed to gain selection for the Lions. He would have been at his peak four years later for the next scheduled tour, only for it to be cancelled because of the war. Miller did play twice for Yorkshire towards the end of the 1930s, totalling five goals.

He had also gained county honours as a schoolboy at Crowle Street School and was shining as an amateur when Hull signed him in 1932. The teenager made his senior-team debut the following year, when he kicked the first three of his many goals for Hull in a 28-8 win at Dewsbury. It was well into the next season before he established himself in the team and then he was a

Freddie Miller in a 1948 Hull squad. From left to right, standing (100 Greats players in capitals): Tattersfield (coach), BOOTH, Evans, Jewitt, Tindall, RYAN, Sullivan, Kavanagh, WATT, CASWELL (trainer). Sitting: MILLER, E. Bedford, Madden, LAWRENCE, Jackson, BOWERS, A. BEDFORD, Sinclair.

regular until the war interfered. He is one of the few Hull players to have made over a century of consecutive appearances, totalling 101 from April 1934 to September 1936.

The unbroken run of appearances included Hull's 21-2 Championship final defeat of Widnes, when Miller kicked a goal. He played in all 47 cup and League matches that season although centre Joe Oliver did most of the goal-kicking. Hull also won the Yorkshire League title in 1935/36 and the two Championships were his only trophy successes, playing in two Yorkshire Cup final defeats. In the last season before the outbreak of war, Miller kicked his first century of goals and got a second in his first post-war season. His total of 103 in 1946/47 put him at the top of goals chart, being then only the second Hull player to achieve the feat. He took over the captaincy in the early post-war years as the club began to build for the future.

A knee injury, which needed a cartilage operation, began to hinder his later years with Hull and he made only five first-team appearances in the last two seasons of the 1940s. His club loyalty continued with the reserve team until he

asked for a transfer to seek more regular first-team opportunities, and in January 1950 Featherstone Rovers signed him for £200. His last game for Hull was in September 1949 and he went out in style, with seven goals in a 44-7 home defeat of Bramley. Miller was thirty-three when he joined Featherstone, injury-prone and obviously long past his best. Many thought Featherstone had wasted money they could ill afford, but it turned out to be one of the best deals they ever did. They were in a depression when he joined them, but his debut brought an end to a run of 12 successive defeats and the start of what old Rovers fans still remember as 'The Miller era'.

Within two years he had virtually booted them to Wembley. He was chaired off the field after his three penalty goals gave Rovers a shock 6-2 semi-final victory over Leigh. Although they were beaten by Workington in the final, Miller completed a memorable 1951/52 with a then club record 101 goals. His twenty-one-year playing career ended in November 1952, and his brief spell at Featherstone was commemorated with the erection of the Freddie Miller Memorial Gate in 1961, following his premature death.

Edgar Morgan
Second row, 1921-26

Season	Apps	Tries	Goals	Pts
1921/22	41	7	0	21
1922/23	33	13	0	39
1923/24	35	6	0	18
1924/25	26	4	0	12
1925/26	42	4	0	12
TOTAL	177	34	0	102

Debut: v. Leeds (A), 27 August 1921
Finals: Rugby League Cup 1921/22 (lost),
1922/23 (lost); Yorkshire Cup 1923/24 (won)

It has always been believed that it takes two years before even the best of rugby union forwards can start to achieve success in the faster and more aggressive rugby league game. Yet former Wales rugby union international flanker Edgar Morgan played for Great Britain against Australia just five weeks after making his rugby league debut with Hull in 1921.

Signed from Llanelli RU, the twenty-five-year-old Morgan played only seven matches before he was pitched in against Australia for the first Test. Eighty minutes later he was being acclaimed as one of the stars of the British pack that laid the foundations for a 6-5 victory. Only seven months earlier he had made the last of his four appearances for Wales RU. He was clearly a natural all-round sportsman, for he had also been a goalkeeper for Llanelli AFC.

Morgan's rapid rugby league progress continued with Hull and at the end of his first season he was playing in the Rugby League Challenge Cup final against Rochdale Hornets. It would have been an even more remarkable climax to his debut season had he not stepped into touch before diving over for what looked like a vital try. The touchdown was disallowed and Rochdale snatched a 10-9 victory despite Hull scoring three tries to two.

Morgan and Hull were in the final again the following year, but there was no hard-luck story this time, as Leeds were easy 28-3 winners. There was still no slowing down Morgan's incredible progress, however, and in only his third season he was made captain of a side packed with born and bred rugby league players, including the great Billy Batten. What's more, he led them to their first Yorkshire Cup final triumph with a 10-4 defeat of Leeds. Alongside him was Bob Taylor, another great Hull forward, and for the next few seasons they formed one of the best second-row partnerships the club has ever had.

That the rugby league game suited Morgan's strong-running style soon became apparent, and the Welshman also relished the fierce exchange of a Humberside derby. One of his most memorable performances came in the Christmas Day clash of 1922, when he stormed through for two tries and played a big part in Hull's 19-6 victory.

Surprisingly, after playing twice for Great Britain as a raw recruit in his first season, he never got another Test call, but he did play five times for Wales and also turned out for Yorkshire against Australia in that astonishing first season.

Steve Norton

Loose forward, 1978-87

Season	Apps	Tries	Goals	Pts
1977/78	14	3	2(2)	11
1978/79	35	15	4(4)	49
1979/80	27	5	1(1)	16
1980/81	35	7	0	21
1981/82	38(1)	8	2(2)	26
1982/83	36(5)	4	0	12
1983/84	21(2)	3	0	12
1984/85	29(3)	1	1(1)	5
1985/86	22(1)	1	0	4
1986/87	26(4)	0	1(1)	1
TOTAL	283(16)	47	11(11)	157

Debut: v. St Helens (H), 29 January 1978
Finals: Rugby League Cup 1979/80 (lost),
1981/82 (drew, 1 try, then won replay), 1982/83
(lost), 1984/85 (lost); Premiership Trophy
1980/81 (lost), 1981/82 (lost), 1982/83 (lost);
Yorkshire Cup 1982/83 (won), 1984/85 (won, 1
try), 1986/87 (lost); John Player Trophy 1981/82
(won); BBC Floodlit Trophy 1979/80 (won)

After only a half-a-dozen matches for Hull in 2001, the Australian Test loose forward Jason Smith was hastily being compared with Steve Norton. There is no doubt that Smith is an outstanding player, but he has a long way to go to replace 'Knocker' in the hearts and minds of Hull fans. Norton was truly a legend in his own lifetime at The Boulevard.

Norton's signing in January 1978 was the catalyst for making Hull a major power in the 1980s. They had to come up with a then world record cash-plus-player (Jimmy Crampton) deal worth £25,000 to prise him from Castleford. It showed Hull meant business about building a great team to lift them out of a depressing period and other stars were quick to follow Norton to The Boulevard.

Arthur Bunting, who had become Hull's coach only three weeks earlier, targeted Norton as a key player in his plans and said at the time of the capture: 'This shows we have our eyes firmly on the future and are prepared to go out and sign class players, not just stop-gaps. Norton will be of great value to our younger players.'

If anything, Norton proved to be an even greater investment than Hull had expected, and his ten years at The Boulevard were the most successful in the club's history. They reached 15 finals and Norton set a club record by playing in 13 of them, plus a replay. He was the captain when Hull met Hull Kingston Rovers in the memorable local derby Wembley final of 1980. In addition to being on the winning side five times, he picked up a Championship medal in 1982/83.

Even in a team packed with internationals, Norton stood out with a succession of top-class performances. He was the ideal loose forward, combining class with vigour, and attacking flair with defensive ruggedness. A good tactical kicker, he could also pop over a drop goal at crucial times in close games.

Highly respected by opponents, he is one of only two players to have been elected by them as the Player of the Year in two separate divisions. He was the top man when Hull won the old Second Division Championship in 1978/79 and he took the major award in 1981/82. As a Hull

Steve Norton on the attack with Trevor Skerrett (left) and Tony Dean in support.

player, he played nine times for Great Britain and went on the 1979 tour of Australia and New Zealand. England called on him three times and he made five appearances for Yorkshire.

At twenty-six he was already an established representative player, having been a Great Britain tourist in 1974, when Hull signed him. Born in Castleford, Norton joined his home town club from local amateur side Fryston Juniors in October 1968. The great Malcolm Reilly was Castleford's loose forward at the time, but after he left for Australia in 1970, Norton came into his own. He made such an impact that he was soon following Reilly Down Under and had two successful close season spells with Manly, helping them to Grand Final success in 1976. The Australian Champions wanted to sign him permanently and though Norton turned them down to return home, his success with Manly made him the target for top clubs in England.

He was clearly aware of this and asked for a transfer in October 1977. Both Leeds and Bradford Northern thought he had agreed to sign for them before Hull clinched the deal. Hull's attendances began to increase immediately, with their best League attendance of the season

(5,822) turning up for his debut. Although Hull lost 18-12 against St Helens to make it nine matches without a win, there was a marked improvement in their play. Norton arrived too late for them to avoid relegation, however, but they swept back to the top sphere in record style after winning all 26 Second Division matches. Hull were on their way to the glory years.

A rare drop in form led Norton to request a transfer in January 1981, but he withdrew it after agreeing to stand down as captain to concentrate on his game. The next few seasons were to be the most successful of his career, apart from a brief spell in 1983 when he had to be talked out of retiring after being troubled by a shoulder injury. He eventually packed up at Hull after a club record benefit season and his last match was in April 1987.

Eighteen months later, Wakefield Trinity coach David Topliss persuaded his former playing colleague at Hull to come out of retirement at thirty-six, but he played only 10 matches with his last in March 1988. Norton had one shot at coaching without success, taking over at struggling Barrow in May 1990 and being sacked ten months later.

Dane O'Hara
Winger, 1981-90

Season	Apps	Tries	Goals	Pts
1981/82	32	15	0	45
1982/83	29	17	0	51
1983/84	36	13	0	52
1984/85	36	22	0	88
1985/86	34	19	0	76
1986/87	40	17	0	68
1987/88	25	7	0	28
1988/89	34	5	0	20
1989/90	10	1	0	4
TOTAL	276	116	0	432

Debut: v. Castleford (H), 27 September 1981
Finals: Rugby League Cup 1981/82 (drew, 1 try),
1982/83 (lost), 1984/85 (lost); Premiership
Trophy 1981/82 (lost), 1982/83 (lost, 1 try),
1988/89 (lost);
Yorkshire Cup 1983/84 (won, 1 try), 1984/85
(won), 1986/87 (lost, 2 tries); John Player Trophy
1981/82 (won), 1984/85 (lost)

No overseas player made more appearances or scored more tries for Hull than Dane O'Hara. The New Zealand Test winger scored 113 tries in 276 matches, spanning the most successful decade in the club's history. Along with James Leuluai and Gary Kemble, who had been colleagues with him on New Zealand's 1980 tour of Britain, O'Hara completed a sensational signing coup by Hull.

Yet he almost signed for arch rivals Hull Kingston Rovers. O'Hara had captained New Zealand against Australia and shone on the 1980s Kiwi tour, when he scored two tries in the 33-10 defeat of Hull at Boothferry Park. As soon as the tour was over, Rovers announced he had agreed to join them, only for Hull to come up with his signature a few days later.

The debuts of O'Hara and Leuluai alongside Kemble, who had already appeared, attracted a crowd of 16,159 to The Boulevard. Ironically, O'Hara's long Hull career almost ended before it had begun, as he suffered a collapsed lung after being kneed by a Castleford player. Fortunately, he made a quick recovery and missed only three matches before becoming an automatic selection for the next eight seasons. In only his eighth match, he picked up a John Player Trophy winners' medal. Near the end of his first season he was playing at Wembley and scored the late try that earned Hull an Rugby League Challenge Cup final replay against Widnes, only for another untimely injury to rule him out of the Cup-winning side. He was back as a loser at Wembley the following year and again in 1985, but had the considerable consolation of being a regular member of Hull's 1982/83 Championship-winning squad.

A strong-running winger, with a powerful finishing style, he had played in the centre for New Zealand and made the occasional appearance there for Hull, most notably in the 1986 Yorkshire Cup final, when he scored two tries in the defeat by Castleford. He continued to play for New Zealand while with Hull and finished with a career total of 36 Test appearances.

O'Hara took over as Hull's captain in his last full season before moving to Doncaster, where injuries restricted him to eight appearances and he played his last match in January 1992.

Joe Oliver

Centre, 1928-38, 1943-45

Season	Apps	Tries	Goals	Pts
1928/29	30	7	37	95
1929/30	41	17	37	125
1930/31	40	7	68	157
1931/32	39	20	42	144
1932/33	39	19	83	223
1933/34	40	18	94	242
1934/35	43	20	83	226
1935/36	40	27	77	235
1936/37	40	11	73	179
1937/38	27	9	63	153
1943/44	26	1	11	25
1944/45	21	0	19	38
TOTAL	426	156	687	1842

Debut: v. St Helens (H), 27 October 1928 (2 goals) Finals: Championship 1935/36 (won, 2 tries and 5 goals)

As their most prolific scorer with club career records of 687 goals and 1,842 points, there is no doubting Joe Oliver's ranking as one of Hull's greatest players. He is also well placed in the other categories, being fifth in both the tries list with 156 and appearances with 426. Oliver's professional career spanned twenty-two years with four clubs from 1923, but it was as a Hull player for twelve seasons that he made his biggest impact. 'Give it to Joe' became a regular cry from the crowd whenever Hull were in a tight spot.

A big, rugged Cumbrian centre or full-back, Oliver joined Hull from Batley via Huddersfield in October 1928 for the then considerable fee of £800. He had just returned from Great Britain's tour Down Under, where he had played in all three Test matches against Australia and one in New Zealand. Oliver later took over as Hull's captain and he had a steadying influence during the Airlie Birds' modest start to the 1930s before he became the driving force that took them to the Championship in 1935/36.

Although Hull obviously played well as a team and had several other outstanding players, it was Oliver who dominated the Championship campaign. He played in 40 of their 47 cup and League matches and headed all three scoring charts with 235 points from 27 tries and 77 goals. The big Cumbrian finished the campaign with probably his best ever performance, as he led Hull to a 21-2 Championship final defeat of Widnes. Oliver set a terrific example, powering in for two tries and kicking five goals. He had also scored a try and two goals in the 13-2 semi-final home defeat of Wigan. Hull's supporters knew who had done most to bring the title back, and they saved their biggest cheer for Oliver when the trophy was paraded at the Guildhall. No doubt there was also a rendering of 'Old Faithful', the old cowboy song that was taken up by their supporters then and remains their battle hymn.

The one blot in a wonderful season for Oliver was his dismissal, along with colleague George Barlow, in the 5-4 Rugby League Challenge Cup third round home defeat against Leeds before a Boulevard record crowd of 28,798. The dismissals cost Hull the game and Leeds went on to win the Cup. In fact,

Joe Oliver with the 1935/36 team and the Yorkshire League Cup. Hull also won the Championship that season. From left to right, back row (100 Greats players in capitals): CASWELL (trainer), Overton, BOOTH, Stead, Dawson, THACKER, L. Barlow, Carmichael. Middle row: G. BARLOW, Wilson, Corner, OLIVER, FIFIELD, MILLER. Front row: HERBERT, Courtney. Inset: ELLERINGTON, Gouldstone.

many Hull fans believed that, but for Leeds, they could have won all four Cups that season. In addition to the Championship, Hull also won the Yorkshire League title, but lost to Leeds in late stages of both the Rugby League Challenge Cup and Yorkshire Cup.

Oliver had two more good years at Hull before his many admirers were stunned by the news in March 1938 that he had crossed the city and signed for the enemy – Hull Kingston Rovers. Within a month he had kicked the two goals that gave Rovers a 13-12 win at The Boulevard. Worse was to follow, as the next season he led the Rovers side that knocked Hull out of the Rugby League Challenge Cup in the first round.

Oliver had two seasons at Rovers before the club disbanded for the duration of the Second World War. He did not play for three seasons and then, at forty years of age, he returned to finish his career with two more seasons at Hull, playing mostly at full-back. His last match was at Dewsbury on 7 April 1945, when he signed off by scoring Hull's only points in a 5-2 defeat.

He returned to Rovers in July 1946 as man-ager-coach and three years later was back at The Boulevard as their trainer-coach for a year to complete almost a quarter of a century at the club.

Surprisingly, he gained no Test honours while at Hull, his four appearances for Great Britain all coming as a Batley player, but he played thrice for England and 27 times for Cumberland as a Hull player, scoring 11 tries and 12 goals for the county side.

Oliver first began to make his mark with Glasson Rangers just after leaving school. There was a brief flirtation as a soccer player with Flimby before he went back to rugby league and was spotted by Huddersfield, with whom he made his senior debut in March 1923. He was an immediate success with the Fartowners and played well over 100 matches for them before moving to Batley for £300 in January 1927. He was now approaching his peak, and it was then that Hull moved in to make one of their most important signings.

Paul Prendiville

Winger, 1978-86

Season	Apps	Tries	Goals	Pts
1978/79	27(4)	25	3	81
1979/80	29(1)	16	8	64
1980/81	36	15	0	45
1981/82	44	18	0	54
1982/83	41	16	30	108
1983/84	9	2	33	74
1984/85	23(5)	1	26	56
1985/86	18(5)	5	13	46
TOTAL	227(15)	98	113	528

Debut: v. Batley (H), 1 October 1978 (1 try and 2 goals) Finals: Rugby League Cup 1979/80 (lost), 1981/82 (drew, then won replay), 1982/83 (lost); Premiership Trophy 1980/81 (lost), 1981/82 (lost); Yorkshire Cup 1982/83 (won, 1 try); John Player Trophy 1981/82 (won)

It took just one pre-season friendly match to convince Hull that they should snap up the unnamed Welsh trialist full-back who had impressed on attack and in defence. The match was an Eva Hardaker Cup match against Hull Kingston Rovers and the 'unknown' player was Paul Prendiville, who kicked five goals in the 28-24 victory. He had scored 320 points for Bynea RU the season before, and was set to join major Welsh club Llanelli until he accepted Hull's offer.

Seven weeks later, he made his competitive debut for Hull, scoring a try and two goals in the 42-9 home defeat of Batley. He was at full-back again, but coach Arthur Bunting switched him to the wing for his next start and discovered a terrific finisher. Prendiville ended his first season as the club's top tryscorer with 25, including four hat-tricks. It was the season in which Hull won all 26 Division Two matches to put them on the threshold of a glorious new era.

Prendiville was to be one of their most consistent performers throughout the glory years, playing in eight finals, including the memorable

Rugby League Challenge Cup replay victory. In their two great campaigns of 1981/82 and 1982/83 when Hull reached all the finals, including winning the Rugby League Challenge Cup plus the Championship, Prendiville missed only six of their 86 matches.

He was not a big or robust winger, but had great determination and plenty of pace, which he used to full effect when going round his opposite number on the outside. His quick, dodging style also enabled him to beat players in a confined space. A typical example of this came in the 1982 Rugby League Challenge Cup semi-final, when he twisted and turned to score Hull's vital last try in the 15-11 defeat of Castleford.

Prendiville played six times for Wales and, though he never appeared in a Test match for Great Britain, he did play for them in a friendly match in Venice.

The Welshman had arrived at Hull with a big reputation as a goal-kicker, but was rarely needed in his early years, as Sammy Lloyd was then sending them over from all distances. Later on, Prendiville was called up as a kicker more often and totalled over 100 goals. He fell only two short of scoring a century of tries for Hull before moving to York in September 1986, having had a long loan spell with Leeds in 1983/84.

Steve Prescott

Full-back, 1998-99, 2001-present

Season	Apps	Tries	Goals	Pts
1998	21	8	20	72
1999	19	7	45(2)	116
2001	26	17	56(1)	179
TOTAL	66	32	121(3)	367

Debut: v. Whitehaven W. (A), 15 February 1998

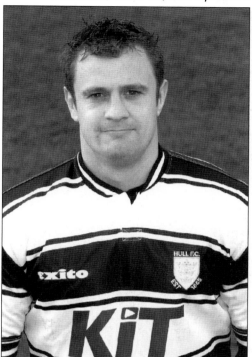

In a few short years, Steve Prescott established himself as one of the best and most popular Hull players of the last decade. The full-back's dashing attacks from the rear, reliability under high kicks and deadly cross-field tackling also made him highly respected by the opposition.

Prescott was signed from St Helens, along with Alan Hunter and Simon Booth, in a deal reckoned to be worth £350,000 before the start of Hull's first Super League campaign in 1998. It was a bold move by Hull, as they sought to make an early impression in the big-time, but only Prescott proved to be value for money. He had been transfer-listed by Saints at £200,000 after requesting a move a year earlier and, even at that price, most Hull fans would feel they had got their money's worth.

So they were far from pleased when Prescott went to Wakefield Trinity for the 2000 season, but he came back the following year and was welcomed with open arms by his fans. This time, with Hull making a strong challenge for honours and finishing third in the Super League, Prescott looked an even more accomplished full-back.

He maintained a high level of consistency throughout the season and reached a peak during Hull's late charge to clinch a top-five place. In one run of seven matches, he totalled 94 points from 8 tries and 31 goals. Such was Prescott's impact over the whole season, the Hull coaching staff chose him as their Player of the Year.

One of Prescott's strongest points is his ability to turn defence into sudden attack and have the pace to go the full length of the field. He did just that in spectacular style against London Broncos in 2001, when snapping up a loose ball and holding off all pursuers in a thrilling race to the line.

The son of former St Helens forward, Eric Prescott, Steve first came to prominence with his father's old club, who had signed him from local Nutgrove amateurs in November 1992. He made his first-team debut a year later and Great Britain Under-21 honours soon followed.

Although senior Great Britain honours have eluded him, Prescott has the unique distinction of holding the match points record for both England and Ireland. He broke the record for his native England with 22 points against France in 1996 and, after changing his allegiance to Ireland, he made it a double, with 14 points for them in a World Cup 2000 match against Samoa. He had qualified for Ireland through an Irish grandparent.

With Hull aiming to regain former glories in the next season or two, they were quick to sign Prescott on a new contract that will keep him at The Boulevard until the end of 2003.

Wayne Proctor

Second row, 1982-88

Season	Apps	Tries	Goals	Pts
1981/82	1(1)	0	0	0
1982/83	19(11)	0	0	0
1983/84	32(13)	5	0	20
1984/85	29(5)	2	0	8
1985/86	16(2)	2	0	8
1986/87	21(8)	3	0	12
1987/88	7(3)	1	0	4
1988/89	5(4)	0	0	0
TOTAL	130(47)	13	0	52

Debut: v. York (H), 16 February 1982
Finals: Yorkshire Cup 1983/84 (won, 1 try),
1984/85 (won); John Player Trophy
1984/85 (lost)

The inclusion of Wayne Proctor in this book may surprise many, but he qualifies with a brief substitute appearance for Great Britain in Papua New Guinea on the 1984 tour. His selection for the tour was also a shock. Although the twenty-year-old second-row forward was not in the original squad, he was brought in as a replacement following the withdrawal of Len Casey because of suspension. The surprise was all the greater because it was thought by many that Hull's other promising young forward of the time, Gary Divorty, should have been selected.

To be fair to Proctor, he had been noted as an outstanding prospect from the moment Hull signed him on his seventeenth birthday. He made good progress, playing for Great Britain Colts and once for Great Britain Under-24s before gaining his call-up for the tour Down Under. His record on tour was also quite good, with 6 tries in 11 matches, including his Test substitution appearance in the last match. But it was mostly down hill from then on, with his only other representative appear-

ance being as a substitute for Great Britain Under-21s.

A product of Hull Colts, Proctor was only eighteen when he made his first-team debut as a substitute midway through the 1981/82 season. Although he did not appear again that season, he played in 13 League matches the following term when Hull won the Championship. He was a regular in Hull's first-team squad the next season, highlighted by his match-clinching try in the 13-2 Yorkshire Cup final defeat of Castleford. Proctor picked up another county Cup winners' medal a year later, but his early promise began to fade and though he continued to challenge for a first-team place for a few more years, it was clear his great expectations were not to be fulfilled.

In December 1989 he was transferred to Doncaster, along with Neil Puckering plus cash, in exchange for their record-breaking winger Neil Turner, in a deal reckoned to be worth over £50,000. He had two seasons at Doncaster and then went on loan to Ryedale-York, where he played two matches before his senior career came to an end in September 1991 while he was still only twenty-seven.

Season	Apps	Tries	Goals	Pts
1906/07	21	5	28	71
1907/08	37	19	8	73
1908/09	35	19	63	183
1909/10	41	18	63	180
1910/11	37	21	47	157
1911/12	43	10	72	174
1912/13	38	4	50	112
1913/14	37	0	65	130
1914/15	42	1	100	203
1919/20	22	1	11	25
1920/21	38	3	6	21
1921/22	41	1	9	21
1922/23	21	0	4	8
1923/24	36	1	5	13
1924/25	11	0	2	4
TOTAL	500	103	533	1375

Debut: v. Leeds (A), 24 November 1906
Finals: Rugby League Cup 1907/08 (lost),
1908/09 (lost), 1909/10 (drew, 1 goal, then lost
replay, 1 goal), 1913/14 (won); Championship
1920/21 (won); Yorkshire Cup 1912/13 (lost, 1
try), 1914/15 (lost), 1920/21 (lost), 1923/24 (won)

Nobody played in more matches for Hull, or had a longer career at the club, than Edward 'Ned' Rogers. The full-back or winger's 500 appearances are more than 40 ahead of his nearest challenger and would have been many more but for the First World War depriving him of four seasons. His nineteen-year career from debut to last match is easily a club record. He is also one of only two players to have scored over 100 tries and 500 goals for the club (the other is Joe Oliver) and he is fourth in the points chart with 1,375. His brother, Greg, also played well over 100 matches for Hull.

Rogers' career covered most of the first quarter of the twentieth century and he played in all of Hull's first seven Cup final appearances, including a replay. War then interrupted before he continued his long service with three more Cup final appearances and completed his haul of winners' medals for all the competitions, including the Yorkshire League Championship. When Hull won the Yorkshire Cup for the first time in 1923, Rogers had been at the club for seventeen years.

Even a full list of Rogers' scoring record and Cup final appearances would convey only a part of his value to Hull over such a long period. Signed from local amateur rugby for only a few pounds, he joined the club just a few years before they began paying out record transfer fees to sign the best players in the Northern Union and beyond. However, none of them could displace the little local lad, who flitted around most back positions until settling at full-back. On the day that Bert Gilbert and Steve Darmody, two major signings from Australia, made their debuts in 1912, it was Rogers who scored all the points, with a try and three goals in the 9-0 defeat of York.

Despite his remarkable run of consistency, Rogers made only two representative appearances, both for Yorkshire. He did play in a trial match before the 1914 Great Britain tour squad to Australia and New Zealand was named, but failed to gain selection. Many

Ned Rogers, at the front, with three more of Hull's 100 Greats. From left to right: Bert Gilbert, Billy Batten and Jack Harrison.

thought he was unlucky to be left out. Among them was club colleague Alf Francis, Hull's sole representative in the squad, who thought Rogers had a better chance than himself of being selected.

'There was good reason for thinking both of us would receive an invitation to tour and especially Ned,' said Francis, who then recalled Hull's recent Rugby League Challenge Cup semi-final defeat of Huddersfield. 'Ned had one of the greatest occasions of his life and his grand goal-getting was the keystone to Hull's success.'

It must have been even more galling for Rogers to read the comment of one of the tour selectors, who said: 'Had Rogers played anything like as well in the past couple of months he would have been a stone certainty to be selected.'

Rogers' disappointment at missing the tour was offset a few weeks later, when he helped Hull to win the Rugby League Challenge Cup for the first time. Rogers had gone within

inches of achieving the feat four years earlier when they drew 7-7 with Leeds. He thought he had scored a late match-winning try when he dived over, only for the touch judge to rule he had hit the corner flag. Hull lost the replay.

Another record held by Rogers is his 31 appearances for Hull in derby matches against Hull Kingston Rovers. He is also one of the few to have scored a derby hat-trick against the old enemy. At 5ft 6in and under 11st, Rogers had to rely on his wits and all-round skills. It was all summed up in this extract from a report after one of his many outstanding performances:

'Rogers carried out his play with matchless precision. He was always cool and generally allowed a fair amount of room in which to work. He did not make a single mistake and his goal-kicking and touch-finding were wonderfully cool and clever. As for tackling, he never missed an opponent.'

Rogers played his last match for Hull on 7 March 1925 in a 2-2 draw at Widnes.

Paul Rose
Second row, 1982-86

Season	Apps	Tries	Goals	Pts
1982/83	39(3)	7	0	21
1983/84	24(2)	3	0	12
1984/85	28(2)	2	0	8
1985/86	4(1)	0	0	0
TOTAL	95(8)	12	0	41

Debut: v. Barrow (A), 22 August 1982 (1 try)
Finals: Rugby League Cup 1982/83 (lost), 1984/85
(lost); Premiership Trophy 1982/83 (lost);
Yorkshire Cup 1982/83 (won, 2 tries), 1984/85
(won); John Player Trophy 1984/85 (lost)

Born in East Hull, and the youngest Hull Kingston Rovers player to make his first-team debut, at 16 years and 9 months, Paul Rose was red and white all the way through for thirteen years – then he signed for the enemy.

Rovers were well compensated, however, as they received a club record fee of £30,000 from Hull in August 1982 for the power-house forward. Within three months, he had become the only man to play for Great Britain as both a Hull and a Hull Kingston Rovers player.

Rose played four times for Britain as a Rovers player and was also a British Lions tourist in 1974, building a reputation as one of the best second-row forwards in the country. He was in the Rovers pack when they beat Hull in the famous Cup final derby at Wembley in 1980 and was later to face his old club in other competition finals.

Although Rose was a little past his best when he signed for Hull, he retained the uncompromising style that made him still a fearsome forward and gained him some notoriety. In the 1983 Cup final against Featherstone Rovers, he became the first player to be sent to the sin bin at Wembley following a high tackle, and in the 1984 Yorkshire Cup final he was sent off for a similar offence, just ninety seconds after going on as a late substitute to face his old Hull Kingston colleagues.

One of his best games for Hull was in the 1982 Yorkshire Cup final when his powerful running brought him two tries and set up another in the 18-7 defeat of Bradford Northern. Despite having a pre-match pain-killing jab for a rib injury, Rose produced a tremendous eighty minutes and was unlucky not to receive the White Rose Trophy as Man of the Match, which went to Bradford full-back Keith Mumby for a great defensive display.

One of his last games for Hull was in the epic 1985 Challenge Cup final against Wigan at Wembley, when the Airlie Birds lost after a thrilling fight-back. He played only four times the following season before ending his long and eventful career in January 1986.

Wilf Rosenberg

Winger, 1961-64

Season	Apps	Tries	Goals	Pts
1961/62	21	15	0	45
1962/63	29	17	0	51
1963/64	27	9	0	27
1964/65	9	1	0	3
TOTAL	86	42	0	126

Debut: v. Bramley (H), 9 December 1961 (2 tries)

Although Wilf Rosenberg had only four seasons at Hull, he showed flashes of just how good a winger he had been for Leeds and as a South African rugby union international centre. What he lacked in size, he made up for in pace and a determination to go for the line, often finishing with a characteristic dive. His spectacular style earned him the nickname of the 'Flying Dentist', having qualified for the profession at Leeds University.

In just under three years at Leeds, Rosenberg had an impressive strike rate of 73 tries in 81 matches, including a club post-war record of 44 in his last full season. Early the next season, he suffered a broken jaw in a game against Hunslet and played only one more match before asking for a transfer. Several clubs were interested and Hull paid £5,750 to sign him. The fee was only £250 short of the club record they had paid a year earlier for another winger, Terry Hollindrake.

Rosenberg scored two tries on his debut for Hull, but all the headlines were about a young trialist winger who scored a hat-trick. The unknown player turned out to be Clive Sullivan.

In the reports of the game, however, was the acknowledgement that Rosenberg scored one of the best tries seen at The Boulevard that season. The *Hull Daily Mail* reported: 'Bramley were on the attack near Hull's 25 when their passing went wrong and Rosenberg had scooped up the ball in a flash. He held off all challengers in a thrilling dash for the line.' It was a typical Rosenberg try. He was always alert to every opportunity and had the pace to turn defence into attack.

Two matches later, the scoring accounts were reversed, with Sullivan getting two tries and Rosenberg racing in for a hat-trick against Bradford Northern. The wing pair revitalised Hull, and totalled 15 tries as the club won five successive matches starting with their debuts. Rosenberg continued his scoring rate at Leeds by finishing the season with 15 tries in 21 matches.

However, an unwanted repeat of his Leeds days came when he again had his jaw broken. It came while he was playing as a guest player for Wakefield Trinity on their brief close season tour of South Africa. Fortunately, it was a hairline break and he was back to score two tries in the pre-season fixture against Hull Kingston Rovers. There was soon another set-back, though, as he needed a cartilage operation. Again he came back with great determination to score eight tries in his last nine matches of the season. Hull began to struggle, however, and Rosenberg's tries started to dry up before he played his last match against his old club Leeds on 19 December 1964 and returned home to South Africa.

Season	Apps	Tries	Goals	Pts
1947/48	27	24	0	72
1948/49	29	13	0	39
1949/50	28	23	0	69
TOTAL	84	60	0	180

Debut: v. Castleford (H), 23 August 1947 (1 try)

There have been few Hull players more idolised than Bruce Ryan. The Australian left-winger is still remembered by his many admirers as the player who was in a class of his own at The Boulevard during the early post-war years. While most of the team were honest grafters struggling to maintain a mid-table position, Ryan stood out as a winger of real quality. As a former Australian sprint champion, he had terrific pace plus a body swerve that swept him in and away from the opposition in smooth, classic style. Add dark, film-star good looks that made him the darling of women supporters, and it is little wonder that Ryan was such a big Boulevard favourite.

He was one of five Australians who played for Hull in the late 1940s, including Test hooker George Watt. But Ryan, who cost £1,750, is the one remembered with awe by those who saw him. Yet it is generally believed he never achieved his full potential, partly because of a lax attitude to training and love of a good social life.

But even if Ryan rarely reached peak fitness, he was still a magnificent athlete at 5ft 10in and over 13st. He was considered a certainty to represent Australia in the 1940 Olympics until war caused their cancellation. He had won the Australian Championships for the 200 and 100 yards that year, clocking 9.7 seconds for the shorter event. Having played rugby union at college, he switched to rugby league in 1941 when he entered the army at eighteen and had his brother as a centre partner. The two of them went

with the same battalion to Papua Guinea where the elder brother was killed in action. Bruce returned to play for Newton in 1943 and was in the side that beat Norths in the Grand Final.

He was in contention for a Test place until a bout of malaria, contracted during a second spell in Papua New Guinea, reduced his weight considerably and dashed any hopes of him playing against the 1946 Great Britain tourists. The following year, former Hull centre Cec Fifield recommended Ryan and scrum-half Duncan Jackson to the club, who signed them immediately. When they arrived at Paragon Station, it was reported that a twenty-deep crowd pressed round the barrier and gave them a Boulevard cheer. It was the start of a wonderful relationship between players and fans, especially for Ryan.

Both made their debuts on the opening day of the season, with Ryan scoring a try in the 27-15 defeat of Castleford on 23 August 1947. There were other hints of the winger's class that were confirmed in the next match when he scored the only try in an 11-7 defeat at Dewsbury. The *Hull Daily Mail* reported: 'The loudest cheer of the day was for Bruce Ryan. During one of the Dewsbury

Bruce Ryan touches down for one of his many brilliant tries.

periods of pressure the Australian took the ball almost on his own line and was away up the field. When Ledgard challenged, Ryan beat him with a classic double-swerve and went over the line three yards ahead of the nearest Dewsbury defender.'

There was better to come, with Ryan's try against the New Zealand tourists a few weeks later still talked about as one of the greatest tries ever scored at The Boulevard. Kiwi defenders were left in his wake, as he swerved in and out on a 75-yard run of grace and splendour.

Despite Hull finishing a modest 12th in the League table, Ryan had an impressive strike rate of 24 tries in 26 matches. Surprisingly, he scored only two hat-tricks for Hull, with his best effort being five in a 44-7 defeat of Bramley in September 1949.

The fans' idolisation was almost matched by the local press and it is said Ryan himself asked journalists to tone it down a bit. But, the story goes, Hull's trainer-coach Eddie Caswell always ended his team talk with 'Get the ball to Ryan.'

Ryan would certainly have scored many more tries for Hull if he had received better service and

the crowd would often encourage him to go inside looking for the ball. It was intended for Roy Francis to provide Ryan with more possession when Hull signed him from Warrington in 1949, but they only played once together before Francis was injured and by the time he had recovered, Ryan had been transferred to Leeds for a then world record £4,750 in April 1950.

The transfer came as a shock to Ryan's adoring fans, although there had been signs that all was not well. He had been suspended for a couple of matches after missing the train for an away match. Though his offer to play without pay was accepted, Ryan remained unsettled and asked for a transfer at the end of the 1949/50 season.

Leeds stepped in immediately to sign him and had high hopes that they would get the best out of the enigmatic winger, but they too would be disappointed. Although his 42 tries in 57 matches over two seasons was another good scoring average, there was always the feeling he had more to offer. Apart from the occasional game, such as when he scored five tries against Hull Kingston Rovers, he remained a great winger who could have been greater.

Garry Schofield
Centre, 1983-87

Season	Apps	Tries	Goals	Pts
1983/84	33(3)	37	57	262
1984/85	34(2)	23	105(1)	301
1985/86	23	15	36(1)	131
1986/87	32(1)	32	1	130
TOTAL	122(6)	107	199(2)	824

Debut: v. Warrington (H), 21 August 1983
Finals: Rugby League Cup 1984/85 (lost);
Yorkshire Cup 1983/84 (won), 1984/85 (won, 4
goals and 1 drop goal), 1986/87 (lost);
John Player Trophy 1984/85 (lost)

Although Garry Schofield was only twenty-two when he left Hull for Leeds in 1987, the young centre was already assured of a place among the club's elite. In just four seasons, he had scored well over 100 tries and just short of 200 goals. He had toured with the British Lions in 1984, played 15 times for Great Britain and once for Yorkshire. A former Great Britain Youth captain, Schofield fulfilled all of his great expectations, going on to make a record-equalling 46 Test and World Cup appearances.

Signed from Hunslet Parkside juniors, the eighteen-year-old centre had just led the Great Britain Youth squad in New Zealand when he was thrust straight into Hull's first team at home to Warrington on 21 August 1983. In only his sixth appearance, three of the others had been as a substitute, he picked up a Yorkshire Cup winners' medal after the 13-2 defeat of Castleford. He had clinched his place in the final with a hat-trick of tries against Leeds. The tries continued to flow and at the end of an extraordinary first senior season, he became the youngest player to finish at the top of the English try chart with 38, including one for Great Britain Under-24s. He also kicked 57 goals to give him a total of 266 points.

Before the end of the season, and less than a year after playing for the international youth side, Schofield made his Great Britain

Test debut. Two months later, he had booked a return trip Down Under with selection for the 1984 tour of Australia and New Zealand. That made him then Britain's youngest ever tourist, as he would not be nineteen until 1 July. Before then he would also become Britain's youngest player to face Australia in a Test match, and he marked it with a try after being moved to scrum-half early in the game when Neil Holding was injured. In the second Test, Schofield scored one of Britain's greatest ever tries, being involved in the 80-yard move three times.

Schofield returned to Hull after the tour as an established Test star with a great future ahead of him. Although much later he was to become a great midfield general playing stand-off for Leeds and Britain, he impressed in his early years with Hull as a try-poaching centre. He was likely to pop up anywhere on the field to finish a move with a try, or he could pluck them out of the air by flashing in for an interception.

Garry Schofield began his long Great Britain career as eighteen-year-old Hull player.

He often produced one when it was most needed, like the match-winner in the Rugby League Challenge Cup third round replay at Widnes in 1985. Winger Kevin James had set it up with a brilliant midfield run before Schofield took over, stumbling from an ankle tap and dashing in from 30 yards on the far left. With Hull fans in a frenzy, Schofield coolly landed the goal from near touch. Despite that effort and starting in all of the Cup rounds, Schofield was relegated to substitute for the final against Wigan. He did not get on to the field until the fifty-eighth minute and by then Hull were 28-12 down. At least he played his part in one of Wembley's greatest finals, as Hull roared back to score three tries, but it was all in vain as they lost 28-24. None of the touchdowns were converted, with Schofield missing two of them.

Although Hull started to go into decline after their last Wembley appearance, Schofield grew in stature, especially at international level. He equalled the Great Britain record for tries in a Test against New Zealand with four in 1985, and the following year became only the fifth British player to score a try in each Test of a series against Australia.

Despite his international success, winners' medals in cup finals were hard to come by. He picked up only three, all in the Yorkshire Cup, and two of those were with Hull. A year after his rapid promotion to play in the 1983 final, he was back as an established centre to kick five goals, including a drop goal, in the 29-12 defeat of Hull Kingston Rovers at Hull City's Boothferry Park.

Schofield's reputation was now just as great in Australia, and he had three successive spells with Balmain during Hull's close seasons, but he never played for Hull again after returning from Australia in 1987. Following a long-standing contractual dispute, he refused to play for Hull and was eventually transferred to Leeds for a then world record £155,000 in October 1997. It had been an acrimonious dispute and many Hull fans never forgave Schofield, giving him a hostile reception whenever he played at The Boulevard. It was a sad end to a marvellous career at Hull, and he always maintained his side of the story was never given in the local press.

Although medals continued to elude him, he had great personal success at Leeds, captaining them for a period. He also captained Britain 13 times and completed a record four tours Down Under. In 1994 he was awarded the OBE for services to rugby league, but things started to go wrong when he left Leeds to become player-coach of Huddersfield in November 1997. He was sacked midway through his first season and had spells with struggling Doncaster and Bramley before playing his last game in August 1999. A few weeks later he joined Redcar Rugby Union Club as player-coach.

Mick Scott
Prop, 1949-63

Season	Apps	Tries	Goals	Pts
1948/49	1	0	0	0
1949/50	11	0	0	0
1950/51	27	6	0	18
1951/52	31	5	0	15
1952/53	39	1	0	3
1953/54	45	4	1	14
1954/55	38	2	0	6
1955/56	42	5	0	15
1956/57	43	4	1	14
1957/58	40	6	0	18
1958/59	44	6	1	20
1959/60	24	2	0	6
1960/61	34	0	0	0
1961/62	27	1	0	3
1962/63	13	1	0	3
TOTAL	459	43	3	135

Debut: v. Rochdale H. (A), 2 April 1949
Finals: Rugby League Cup 1958/59 (lost),
1959/60 (lost); Championship 1955/56 (won),
1956/57 (lost), 1957/58 (won, 1 try);
Yorkshire Cup 1953/54 (lost), 1945/55 (lost),
1955/56 (drew, then lost replay), 1959/60 (lost)

Second in Hull's all-time list of appearances with 459, Mick Scott was a cornerstone of their mighty pack of the 1950s. He was the first of that famous set to make their debuts, packing down as an eighteen-year-old for just one match late in the 1948/49 season. He was in the second row then, but it was as a pile-driving prop that he established himself in the Hull team over the next fifteen years.

He also captained Hull in the mid-1950s, and though he was best known for leading by example, he made one of the most crucial on-field decisions ever made in the club's history. It came two minutes from the end of the 1956 Championship final at Manchester City's Maine Road ground. Halifax were leading 9-8 when Hull received a penalty close to the opposition's line and near touch. The unlimited possession rule was in operation then, and the natural instinct would have been to take a tap penalty and go for a try. It looked as if Hull were going

to do that when Scott grabbed the ball and tossed it to Colin Hutton for a shot at goal. Hutton justified his captain's faith to bang it over and bring the Championship back to Hull for the first time in twenty years.

Scott had handed over the captaincy to Johnny Whiteley by the time of the 1958 Championship final, but he was still a driving force and played a major role in the 20-3 defeat of Workington Town. It was his long, well-judged pass that sent in Brian Cooper for Hull's first try, and late in the game the big prop nimbly stepped round Workington stand-off Harry Archer to go over for a decisive late touchdown.

Scott shared with Whiteley the feat of playing in all 10 finals – including a Yorkshire Cup replay – which Hull reached from 1953 to 1960. He was a central figure in the explosive incidents of the 1955 county final against Halifax when twice a scrum broke up with a prop from either side suffering a facial wound. Nobody was penalised, but Scott was always one of the usual suspects when the going was at its roughest. Yet, he could also produce a subtle touch when needed and was sur-

Mick Scott puts in a kick during the 1960 Rugby League Challenge Cup final against Wakefield Trinity at Wembley.

prisingly quick on his feet for such a hefty forward. Despite being born close to The Boulevard ground, Scott never played rugby league as a schoolboy and was a centre-half for the Wawne Street School soccer side. He continued with soccer at Mersey Street youth club before deciding to give rugby a go with Boulevard Juniors, then Hull's nursery side. After just a year, he had a pre-season trial for the senior club and signed for Hull in August 1948.

Eight reserve-team matches later, he was playing for England Under-21s and captained them in their next match. He then scored two tries playing for a British Empire XIII against a Welsh XIII as part of the 1951 Festival of Britain celebrations. Full international honours followed with his debut for England at nineteen. It was remarkable progress for a youngster who had come into the game so late, but though he continued to improve and became one of the best props of the decade, he made only two more appearances for England and none for Great Britain. He did play in a 1954 tour trial, but was not selected after facing all-time great Alan

Prescott. If international calls were scarce, county selection was almost automatic and his 16 appearances for Yorkshire are exceeded by only one Hull player, Harry Taylor with 19. Scott's failure to gain even one Test cap surprised many, and after his 1958 Championship final display, the *Hull Daily Mail's* Kingstonian wrote: 'A player who took the eye particularly was big Mick Scott, the burly Hull front row forward who played a superb game. What a pity he is not going to Australia this summer, for on his last two displays Mick has looked the best field-side man in the game.'

Scott continued as a regular in Hull's front row until the early 1960s when his appearances became less frequent. Unsettled, he asked for a move and had been on the transfer list at £1,000 for a year when he went to Rochdale Hornets in July 1963. His last match for Hull was at Leeds on 1 May 1963. He played in 32 matches for Rochdale in 1963/64 before retiring at the end of the season.

Scott was only thirty-seven when he was killed in an accident on Hull docks in June 1968.

Season	Apps	Tries	Goals	Pts
1980/81	33	10	0	30
1981/82	38(2)	3	0	9
1982/83	27(2)	2	0	6
1983/84	20	2	0	8
1984/85	14(1)	0	0	0
1985/86	22(1)	1	0	4
TOTAL	154(6)	18	0	57

Debut: v. Featherstone R. (A), 17 August 1980 (1 try) Finals: Rugby League Cup 1981/82 (drew, then won replay), 1982/83 (lost); Premiership Trophy 1980/81 (lost), 1981/82 (lost), 1982/83 (lost); Yorkshire Cup 1982/83 (won), 1983/84 (won); John Player Trophy 1981/82 (won)

Hull paid Wakefield Trinity a then world record £40,000 for Trevor Skerrett in June 1980 and never regretted a penny of it. He was a cornerstone of their pack during the club's glorious years of the early 1980s, confirming his reputation as one of the hardest prop or second-row forwards in the game. Hunslet-born, Skerrett signed for Wakefield Trinity in 1973 and first came to the fore when playing for Wales against the 1978 Australian tourists. Having Welsh grandparents qualified him for Wales and he went on to make seven appearances for them, three as a Hull player. He also captained Wales in his last international match.

A 1979 Great Britain tourist to Australasia, Skerrett was one of the few players to impress on a disappointing tour, and when he requested a transfer the following year, Hull moved in to add him to their already powerful pack. He produced a typical hard, grafting performance to win the Man of the Match award when Hull beat Hull Kingston Rovers in the 1981/82 John Player Trophy final, and also figured prominently in their Rugby League Challenge Cup success that season.

He played in nine finals, including the cup replay of 1982, and earned a Championship medal in 1982/83. His international career was also going well until 1984 when he received his greatest honour and biggest disappointment. Called upon to be the first Hull player to captain a Great Britain squad Down Under, he was forced to pull out with a knee injury that was to trouble him for the rest of his career, but he battled back to regain his Great Britain place and played in six Test matches as a Hull player plus three games for Yorkshire.

Another injury blow came when he was ruled out of Hull's pack for the Rugby League Challenge Cup final at Wembley in 1985. Three weeks later he asked for a transfer after becoming unsettled and was listed at £75,000, but he did not move until September 1986 when he joined Leeds. It was part of a three-player deal with Hull's Andy Gascoigne also going to Leeds and Kevin Dick joining the Airlie Birds. Leeds also paid a small fee.

Skerrett had two seasons at Leeds and another two with Keighley, where he finished his senior career at end of the 1988/89 season. He then went back to his old amateur club, Bison, and a few months later captained the Leeds side to Yorkshire ARL Cup final success.

Peter Sterling

Scrum-half, 1983-84, 1984-85

Season	Apps	Tries	Goals	Pts
1983/84	8	1	0	4
1984/85	28(2)	8	0	32
TOTAL	36(2)	9	0	36

Debut: v. Wakefield T. (A), 4 December 1983
Finals: Rugby League Cup 1984/85 (lost);
Yorkshire Cup 1984/85 (won);
John Player Trophy 1984/85 (lost)

An Australian legend in his own lifetime, Peter Sterling totalled only 36 appearances in two spells at Hull – easily the fewest number of matches by any of the *100 Hull Greats*, but the scrum-half supreme made such an impact in such a short time that he will long be remembered as one of the greatest players to play for the club.

His times with Hull came during a career that saw him make 18 Test appearances for Australia, tour twice with the Kangaroos and play a major role in Parramatta winning four Premierships. He was at his peak when Hull pulled off a sensational coup by getting him to sign a short-term contract to play just eight matches in 1983/84. At about the same time, Wakefield Trinity signed another Australian legend, Wally Lewis, and the Kangaroos halfback pair made their English club debuts in opposition at Wakefield on 4 December 1983.

Hull's only loss during Sterling's brief stay was a narrow defeat at Wigan and his immediate success resulted in him agreeing to having almost a full season the following term.

It turned out to be a memorable one, with Sterling inspiring Hull to three finals. He won the White Rose Trophy as Man of the Match in the Yorkshire Cup final defeat of Hull Kingston Rovers, who gained revenge by defeating Hull in the John Player Special Trophy final.

Then came the Rugby League Challenge Cup. After helping Hull to comfortable wins in the first two rounds, Sterling missed the home tie against Widnes when they were held to a 6-6 draw, but he was back to inspire them to a great replay win before rising to even greater heights in the semi-final. After being held to another draw, against Castleford, Sterling increased the tempo in the replay and, despite taking a severe battering, played a major role in a memorable victory. On to Wembley, and Sterling produced yet another outstanding performance, but this time it was all in vain, as Wigan held out to win one of the greatest finals of all time.

That was Sterling's last appearance for Hull and though he agreed to return in 1987, the deal fell through. Leeds appeared to have captured him two years later, only for a bad ankle injury to dash their hopes. He then developed a shoulder problem and, after another dislocation while playing for Parramatta, retired in April 1992.

Season	Apps	Tries	Goals	Pts
1919/20	26	27	4	89
1920/21	34	38	9	132
1921/22	42	17	10	71
1922/23	42	26	6	90
1923/24	39	25	9	93
1924/25	39	16	1	50
TOTAL	222	149	39	525

Debut: v. Wakefield T. (H), 18 October 1919 (1 try) Finals: Rugby League Cup 1921/22 (lost), 1922/23 (lost); Championship 1920/21 (won, 1 try); Yorkshire Cup 1920/21 (lost), 1923/24 (won)

Of all the players Hull have recruited from rugby union, one of the very best was Billy Stone. He had played for the Gloucestershire Regiment and Gloucester Rugby Union Club when Hull signed him shortly after the First World War. A team colleague, Bill Davis, signed for Leeds at about the same time after they had outbid Hull for the forward's services. Although Davis went on to have a longer rugby league career than Stone, he never made the same impact.

At the end of his first season, Stone's remarkable quick progress – he had scored 27 tries, including three hat-tricks – was recognised when he was selected for the Great Britain tour of Australia and New Zealand. The following season he finished as the top tryscorer with 41, including three in two matches for England. His nearest challenger, Joe Brittain of Leeds, was 19 tries behind. Stone ended the season with a scoring blitz, touching down in all of Hull's last seven games for a total of 19, including a personal best of five in a match.

Signed originally as a centre, Stone often partnered the great Billy Batten in the middle during his first season and outscored the Hull legend 27 tries to 21. They were centre partners when Hull lost 2-0 to Hull Kingston Rovers in the 1921 Yorkshire Cup final, but Stone was on the wing and scored a vital try when they gained a 16-14 revenge victory in the Championship final at the end of the season. He continued to alternate between centre and wing until 1922/23 when he settled on the right flank.

Reports at the time refer to him as: 'An outstanding all-round player with a baffling corkscrew run and brilliant dashes. He makes beautiful passes and has a quick measure of the situation. He also has speed, swerve, a great sidestep and an uncanny knack of anticipating his opponents' moves, allied to courageous defensive play and a deadly tackle. Once, opposing Cecil Blinkhorn, the great Australian wingman never passed Stone on a single occasion.'

That he was a player with natural ability was confirmed on the 1920 tour Down Under. Despite having switched codes only six months earlier, Stone was one of the stars of the tour. Stone finished with 24 tries in 17 matches, the try total remaining a tour record for twenty-six years. He was on the wing for the first two Test matches against Australia and then moved into the centre for the final game when the

Billy Stone and four more of Hull's 100 Greats, as seen by cartoonist Ern Shaw in 1923. From left to right: Eddie Caswell, Stan Whitty, Stone, Billy Batten and Jim Kennedy.

Ashes had already been lost. Stone stood out with two tries and he also kicked a goal. The first try typified his alertness and speed as he picked up a loose ball and raced 80 yards to the line, unopposed.

Stone was an even greater success in New Zealand, where he played a major role in helping Britain win all three Test matches, scoring a hat-trick in the first and grabbing two more in the second. The following year, Stone nipped in for a typical and decisive opportunist's try in the 6-5 first Test defeat of Australia. He also played in the next Test, but that was to be the last of his eight appearances for Great Britain, all of them within two years of turning professional. His eight tries in as many Test matches reflects his brief, but impressive contribution.

He had a similar record for England with six tries in six matches and he scored a try in a 1924 tour trial match, but was not selected for the Down Under trip. To complete his extraordinary scoring average in representative matches, the former Gloucestershire Rugby Union player scored a try in his one appearance for Yorkshire when they lost to the 1921 Australian tourists at Wakefield. That's a total of 16 tries in 16 representative matches.

More honours would probably have followed had his career not been cut prematurely short by a back injury sustained at Halifax towards the end of the 1924/25 season. It was not thought to be serious at the time, and he played in the three remaining matches of the campaign, but the match at home to Hunslet was to prove the last of his career as he was placed in a plaster cast for the next three years, back in his native Forest of Dean where he had once been the village blacksmith. Once he regained near full fitness, he returned to Hull where he was a supervisor in the despatch department of caterers William Jackson and Son Ltd for almost thirty years. In his later years, he became a championship-grade bowls player of some distinction, but he is still remembered as a rugby league player who thrilled The Boulevard crowds and others much farther afield with his exciting style.

Richard 'Charlie' Stone

Prop, 1978-83

Season	Apps	Tries	Goals	Pts
1978/79	38	4	0	12
1979/80	38(2)	1	0	3
1980/81	37(2)	2	0	6
1981/82	38(2)	0	0	0
1982/83	34	1	0	3
1983/84	6(1)	0	0	0
TOTAL	191(7)	8	0	24

Debut: v. Bramley (A), 20 August 1978
Finals: Rugby League Cup 1979/80 (lost),
1981/82 (drew, then won replay), 1982/83 (lost);
Premiership Trophy 1980/81 (lost), 1981/82
(lost), 1982/83 (lost); Yorkshire Cup 1982/83
(won); John Player Trophy 1981/82 (lost);
BBC Floodlit Trophy 1979/80 (won)

After signing ball-playing forwards Vince Farrar and Steve Norton, Hull looked for a hard-working forager as they sought to build a mighty pack that would blast them back into the top division. Charlie Stone fitted that job description perfectly and they paid just under Featherstone Rovers' asking price of £15,000 to sign him in July 1978 after he had asked for a transfer.

Rovers had signed him from Pontefract Rugby Union Club in 1970 and he became a major force as they won the Cup at Wembley and lifted the Championship. Within five years, he had helped Hull to the same trophies and more.

Hull's first target was achieved in record style as they gained promotion by winning all 26 matches, with Stone missing only one. He formed the ideal second-row partnership with Sammy Lloyd, who was more of a runner, while Stone tackled everything in sight. Stone gained further reward when he and Norton were the only players outside the top division to be selected for Great Britain's 1979 tour of Australasia. He played in 12 matches on tour, but failed to make the Test side and they remained his only representative appearances as a Hull player.

The following season brought Stone the first of his 10 final appearances with Hull – a BBC TV Floodlit Trophy defeat of Hull Kingston Rovers, who got their revenge at the end of the season with their famous Wembley victory. The fierce local rivalry continued and Stone, who had moved up to the front row, was captain when Hull beat Rovers in the 1981/82 John Player Trophy final. He was sent off for butting four minutes before the final whistle, but returned to lift the cup.

Another butting incident cost Hull more dearly the following season, when Stone was penalised for the offence just three minutes from the end of the Cup final at Wembley, and Steve Quinn added the goal to give Featherstone Rovers a shock victory. Ironically, Stone returned to Featherstone the following October in a novel rent-a-player scheme introduced by Hull. He played 14 matches at Featherstone before moving to Bradford Northern in September 1984. Although no fee was reported, he had been on the list at £20,000. His one season with Bradford was his last in senior rugby.

Clive Sullivan
Winger, 1961-74, 1981-83, 1984-85

Season	Apps	Tries	Goals	Pts
1961/62	17	13	0	39
1962/63	8	6	0	18
1963/64	7	7	0	21
1964/65	27	18	0	54
1965/66	37	23	0	69
1966/67	28	28	0	84
1967/68	20	17	0	51
1968/69	17	12	0	36
1969/70	39	21	0	63
1970/71	41	33	0	99
1971/72	40	30	0	90
1972/73	29	18	0	54
1973/74	30	21	0	63
1981/82	9(4)	1	0	3
1982/83	2	2	0	6
1984/85	1(1)	0	0	0
TOTAL	352(5)	250	0	750

Debut: v. Bramley (H), 9 December 1961 (3 tries)
Finals: Rugby League Cup 1981/82 (won replay);
Yorkshire Cup 1969/70 (won, 1 try)

When an unnamed trialist winger scored three tries on his debut for Hull in December 1961, a bright future was predicted for the eighteen-year-old Welshman, but no one could have foreseen the wonderful playing career that lay ahead for Clive Sullivan. He went on to score a record 250 tries for Hull, including a club record seven in one match at Doncaster. He captained Great Britain to World Cup success in 1972 and finished with 406 touchdowns in a twenty-three-year career with four clubs.

The popular 'Sully' was also one of the few players to be revered by both Hull and Hull Kingston Rovers fans, for he was the only one to score a century or more tries for both clubs and also to win an Rugby League Challenge Cup winners' medal with each. This rare bonding was acknowledged following his premature death when the city's major new road linking east and west was named the Clive Sullivan Way.

Sullivan was a winger in the classic mould. Built on thoroughbred lines, he had pace to match and there was no better sight in rugby league than Sullivan in full flight for the line.

Given only an inch or two to spare, he could beat his opposite number on the outside and race clear of the fastest cover. But, rare in wingers of his classic attacking style, he was also a keen defender who would streak across the field to bring down a runaway opponent.

There were hints of Sullivan's all-round ability on his memorable debut when he raced in for a hat-trick in the 29-9 home defeat of Bramley. Wilf Rosenberg, the former South African rugby union international signed from Leeds, also made his debut on the other wing that day and scored two tries, but it was the unnamed trialist who hit the headlines. One report read: 'In the first minute, the young coloured RU man with an action resembling the great Billy Boston sped down the wing in fine style and only a last ditch tackle by Maori full-back Wilson halted his progress. From then on he was constantly in the picture and before the game ended had run in a brilliant hat-trick of tries, the last after a 50-yard dash that brought the house down.' Sullivan's first two tries came from well-timed passes from

Johnny Whiteley, Hull's great loose forward who had moved to centre during the game when Jack Kershaw went off injured. The youngster could not have had a better guardian centre.

Two days later, Hull announced they had signed the young winger from Cardiff's Tiger Bay. It was later revealed that he had played a trial match for Bradford Northern reserves, but did not impress enough to be called back. It was then that John Harker, a Hull referee who had been a touch judge at the match, told the youngster not to give up and arranged a trial with Hull. The rest is history. The only snag with his signing for Hull is that he was in the army with the Royal Signals and was not discharged until 1964. Although he managed to play occasional games while on leave, his career was also hampered by severe injuries, suffered both on the field and in a car accident.

Once he was back playing first-team rugby, his progress increased and he made his Test debut for Great Britain three years later. Despite scoring an early try against France at Carcassonne, Sullivan was having a poor game until he scored a brilliant match-winning try three minutes from the end. It was the start of an outstanding career with Britain, making 17 appearances and being a 1970 tourist – all as a Hull player, as were five of his appearances for Wales. He also became the first black player to captain Britain and his greatest international moment came when he led them to World Cup success in 1972 after scoring a vital 80-yard try in the final against Australia. Sullivan had now attained national fame, extremely rare for a rugby league player, and he became the first to be the subject of television's *This is Your Life*. Greater acclaim was to follow with the award of the MBE in January 1974.

At club level, however, the only medal he won in his first spell at the club came with the 12-9 defeat of Featherstone Rovers in the 1969 Yorkshire Cup final. Although he scored a try, it is the one he missed that is remembered most. It came when he slipped over the dead-ball line as he turned to move towards the posts. Sullivan became Hull's player-coach in 1973/74, but quit in March 1974 following a dispute over his testimonial. 'Sully' then shocked his fans when he transferred to arch rivals Hull Kingston Rovers for the start of the following season. At thirty-

Clive Sullivan on the way to scoring a try at Bradford Northern in 1966.

one, Sullivan was just beginning a highly successful new era as he shared in Rovers' many successes over the next six seasons, including their Wembley defeat of Hull in 1980. That was his last match for Rovers as he signed for Oldham. A broken arm restricted his appearances at Oldham and he returned to Hull in July 1981 as their A-team coach, although also playing a few first-team matches. One of those matches was the 1982 Rugby League Challenge Cup final replay defeat of Widnes when, at thirty-nine, he replaced the injured Dane O'Hara.

Sullivan lost the A-team job in a coaching shake-up in December 1982 and became Doncaster's player-coach the following March. A year later, he quit and returned to Hull, offering to play if ever they needed him. Sullivan played his last match as a substitute at Bradford on 23 April 1985 at the age of forty-two. Tragically, he died of cancer in October that year. His son, Anthony, followed him as an outstanding winger with Hull Kingston Rovers, St Helens, Wales and Great Britain.

Cyril Sykes
Second row, 1956-67

Season	Apps	Tries	Goals	Pts
1956/57	21	4	0	12
1957/58	21	8	15	54
1958/59	38	5	27	69
1959/60	41	11	12	57
1960/61	38	9	1	29
1961/62	13	3	0	9
1962/63	24	6	1	20
1963/64	18	2	0	6
1964/65	21(1)	3	0	9
1965/66	16(1)	0	0	0
1966/67	30(1)	4	4	20
1967/68	18	1	2	7
TOTAL	299(3)	56	62	292

Debut: v. St Helens (H), 15 September 1956
Finals: Rugby League Cup 1958/59 (lost);
Championship 1956/57 (lost), 1957/58 (won);
Yorkshire Cup 1959/60 (lost), 1967/68 (lost)

One of the best Hull players never to gain representative honours, that was Cyril Sykes. He never even gained a county cap. Yet he played twelve years for Hull, mostly in the second row, and was a member of the mighty pack that won the Championship in 1957 and powered to Wembley two years later. Perhaps he did not have the power of Harry Markham, the man he replaced, or the ball-playing skills of his second-row partner for many years, Bill Drake, but he was a tireless worker with a high level of consistency. He was also an occasional goal-kicker.

A local lad, Sykes excelled at other sports before signing for Hull. He had been a useful soccer player at school and was an even better rugby union player in the Army. The Army also introduced him to skiing while on National Service in Austria, and he made such quick progress that he was on the shortlist for the Olympics until being ruled out by a mouth abscess. After being demobbed, he tried his hand at rugby league and it took just six matches with the reserves to convince Hull to sign him.

Although Hull had a pack of internationals, it did not take Sykes long to force his way into it, and at the end of his first season, he played in the Championship final against Oldham. Unfortunately, he was the central figure in an incident that turned the game and led to Oldham winning 15-14, but Sykes was entirely blameless as the referee penalised him for not getting up to play-the-ball, realising too late that he was injured. Hull were leading 11-5 at the time, with thirty minutes left, but Bernard Ganley banged over the goal from near halfway and Oldham went on to victory.

Sykes continued to be a regular in the pack and helped Hull to Wembley finals in 1959 and 1960, but he missed the latter because of a shoulder injury after playing in 41 matches that season. Having played with Hull through the good times, he stayed with them through some tougher years in the 1960s. Eleven years after making his debut, he had a reminder of his best years when he played in the Yorkshire Cup final defeat against Hull Kingston Rovers in October 1967. The following month he moved to Doncaster, where he had a spell as player-coach, before ending his long playing career in February 1971.

Season	Apps	Tries	Goals	Pts
1919/20	17	11	0	33
1920/21	35	20	0	60
1921/22	35	22	0	66
1922/23	37	25	0	75
1923/24	29	14	0	42
1924/25	20	9	0	27
1925/26	35	32	0	96
1926/27	37	16	0	48
1927/28	37	5	0	15
1928/29	19	8	0	24
1929/30	6	2	0	6
TOTAL	307	164	0	492

Debut: v. Wakefield T. (A), 31 January 1920
Finals: Rugby League Cup 1921/22 (lost, 1 try),
1922/23 (lost); Championship 1919/20 (won),
1920/21 (won, 2 tries); Yorkshire Cup 1920/21
(lost), 1923/24 (won), 1927/28 (lost)

In an age when forwards were regarded as labourers for the backs, second-rower Bob Taylor was a tryscoring phenomenon. His 36 tries in 1925/26, including four for England, stood as a record for a forward until it was broken by Leeds' Bob Haigh's 40 in 1971 and later Ellery Hanley's 41 in 1995. Taylor's career total of 164 tries for Hull is a record by a forward for the club, with only three wingers ahead of him in the overall list. He also held the joint club record of six tries in a match, until that great winger Clive Sullivan went one better forty-seven years later.

Yet for all his extraordinary tryscoring feats, Taylor still looked the typical forward of the era. He was around 6ft, weighed over 15st and appeared to have more paunch than power, but give Taylor the ball and his legs became pistons, powering him forward at an amazing pace for such a big man. Sporting a Roman nose, he presented a terrifying sight for the opposition when he was in full charge.

Again appearances were deceptive. Many an ogre on the field is glibly described as a gentle giant off it, but in Taylor's case it was undeniably true, for he was a religious man and a member of the Salvation Army. It was said: 'He slayed 'em

on a Saturday and saved 'em on a Sunday.' Jim Sullivan, the legendary Wigan full-back, used to tell a story of how Taylor had wreaked havoc against them at The Boulevard. Later, as the Wigan team was going to Paragon Station after the match, they passed a Salvation Army Band and the conductor smiled at them. It was Bob Taylor.

Born in Barrow, Taylor played for his home town club before the First World War and did not sign for Hull until 1920. He joined them at the height of their post-war power and helped them to win the Championship in both of his first two seasons at the club. The second of the Championship final victories was a personal triumph for Taylor, as he powered in for two vital tries that gave Hull a 16-14 victory over arch rivals Hull Kingston Rovers at Headingley. It was ample revenge for Hull and particularly for Taylor, who had had a try disallowed in the 2-0 Yorkshire Cup final defeat by Rovers earlier in the season. Taylor's efforts were also in vain when Hull lost 10-9 in the 1922 Rugby League Challenge Cup final against Rochdale Hornets,

TAYLOR MOVING EVANS AND EARTH TO SCORE

Bob Taylor was a favourite of cartoonist Ern Shaw. Here he shows how Taylor smashed into Batley's Evans to score in a 1920 cup tie.

despite scoring three tries to two. He crowned an outstanding game with a magnificent late touchdown that gave Hull a chance of snatching victory, but Billy Stone was off-target with a difficult conversion attempt.

Taylor's club record-equalling six tries in a match came in a 69-11 home defeat of Wakefield Trinity on 15 January 1921 when the opposition found him virtually unstoppable. Five years later, every team found him almost impossible to stop as he charged to his record 36 tries in a season. So did Wales and Other Nationalities as he scored two tries against each. Taylor finished the season second only to Wigan's international winger Johnny Ring, who was way out in front with 63. Taylor maintained his high tryscoring average at representative level with a dozen in thirteen appearances. He totalled two in two appearances for Great Britain, seven in seven for England and three in two for Lancashire. His three for Lancashire was a hat-trick in a rampag-

ing performance against Cumberland, who were beaten 46-9. Surprisingly, Taylor played in only two Test matches for Great Britain but was on the winning side each time. Although he did not score against Australia in 1922, he had a hand in both of Britain's tries that brought them an Ashes-winning 6-0 victory. Five years later, he ended his representative career with two tries for Great Britain in a 28-20 first Test defeat of New Zealand.

Although Taylor's representative days ended in 1927 he continued to give Hull sterling service for a few more years, confirming his ranking as one of the most popular players to play for the club. Even when the tries started to dry up, he managed to turn back the clock with a hat-trick against Dewsbury in 1928 when he had been playing first-team rugby for nearly twenty years. He finally called it a day a year later, playing his last match in an 8-4 Yorkshire Cup second round home defeat against Hunslet.

Harry Taylor
Full-back, 1898-1910

Season	Apps	Tries	Goals	Pts
1897/98	15	0	0	0
1898/99	26	2	0	6
1899/1900	26	2	2	10
1900/01	27	0	0	0
1901/02	24	0	0	0
1902/03	33	0	0	0
1903/04	24	0	1	2
1904/05	31	0	0	0
1905/06	32	3	1	11
1906/07	26	1	1	5
1907/08	30	0	0	0
1908/09	34	0	0	0
1909/10	33	1	0	3
1910/11	2	0	0	0
TOTAL	363	9	5	37

Debut: v. Bradford (A), 1 January 1898
Finals: Rugby League Cup 1907/08 (lost),
1908/09 (lost), 1909/10 (drew)

To Hull-born Harry Taylor went the honour and distinction of being the first ever captain of Great Britain. A dominant figure as Hull's full-back at the start of the twentieth century, he led Britain in all three Test matches against the inaugural New Zealand tourists of 1907/08.

Taylor's value to Britain was summed up in a match report following the 14-6 first Test victory: 'The Hull man created two tries with brilliant play and gave an exhibition throughout that was quite the leading feature of the game. Some of Taylor's saves were really wonderful and his all-round play was magnificent. He also realises that under Northern Union rules there are possibilities open to a custodian that would be regarded as risky play in the rugby union game, and he makes the most of those possibilities.'

Taylor's career spanned the transformation of the game from basically 15-a-side rugby union to the new faster and more open code, which suited his approach. His status reached its peak in 1907/08, as he also captained England and Yorkshire in addition to leading Hull to their first appearance in a Cup final. The defeat against Hunslet was the beginning of a hat-trick of losses in the Rugby League Challenge Cup final, although Taylor missed the 1910 replay after playing in the 7-7 draw against Leeds. In fact, Taylor never gained a winner's medal during his fourteen seasons with Hull, and Britain lost the series against New Zealand when he captained them. However, time and again he was praised for his valour in defeat. Yet he was not a regular pointscorer, totalling only nine tries and five goals in a long career with Hull. Wholly dependable, steadfast in defence and a great inspiration to his team is how he comes across in a succession of match reports.

There was little international rugby league played during Taylor's early years with Hull, but he did manage two appearances for England in addition to his three Test matches for Britain. He also made 19 appearances for Yorkshire and played in nine county trial matches.

Hull have had many outstanding full-backs over the last century or so, and it was Taylor who set the standard during the game's infancy.

Laurie Thacker

Prop, 1933-46

Season	Apps	Tries	Goals	Pts
1933/34	25	2	0	6
1934/35	2	0	0	0
1935/36	36	9	0	27
1936/37	39	2	0	6
1937/38	36	5	0	15
1938/39	40	9	0	27
1939/40	24	3	0	9
1940/41	22	8	0	24
1941/42	22	3	0	9
1942/43	2	0	0	0
1943/44	1	0	0	0
1944/45	9	1	0	3
1945/46	20	2	0	6
TOTAL	**278**	**44**	**0**	**132**

Debut: v. Dewsbury (A), 2 September 1933
Finals: Championship 1935/36 (won);
Yorkshire Cup 1938/39 (lost)

One of the hardest forwards to play for Hull was Laurie Thacker, and he also proved his toughness off the field as a commando with the British Army. He suffered a leg wound in action during the Second World War, but regained fitness to play several more games for Hull.

Signed from local amateur club Marlborough in 1933, he made his first-team debut soon after and became a regular member of the squad for the rest of the season. Injury restricted him to only two appearances the following season, and he then came back to play a major role in Hull's momentous 1935/36 season. He played in 36 of Hull's 47 matches of a hectic season that finished with the Airlie Birds winning the Championship and the Yorkshire League title.

Although Hull had a top-class back division with the likes of Freddie Miller, Joe Oliver and Dickie Fifield, it was their forwards whom the opposition feared most. Thacker led the forward barrage, repeatedly taking the ball up in the days when a team could retain possession for long periods. As a hefty prop, he also used his strength to great effect in the scrums to give

his hooker a big advantage. It was that sort of power that gave Hull total command in the Championship final when they beat Widnes 21-2.

Thacker was at his peak in the last peace-time season before the outbreak of war when Hull reached the Yorkshire Cup final, only to go down 18-10 to Huddersfield. He played in both of England's matches that season and also for Yorkshire, but his hopes of more representative honours faded as the war clouds gathered. In all, he played four times for both Yorkshire and England.

He would have been a strong contender for the scheduled tour of Australia and New Zealand in the summer of 1940 had there not been a greater battle for Britain to be fought. Thacker went off to join the fight in France and Germany before being wounded. On returning to Hull, he fought his way back to fitness and managed to play in a dozen matches in the last three wartime seasons. His vast experience was called on more often in Hull's post-war first season before he played his last match at home to Leeds on 2 May 1946.

Keith Tindall
Prop, 1972-84

Season	Apps	Tries	Goals	Pts
1971/72	1(1)	0	0	0
1972/73	9(1)	0	0	0
1973/74	13(6)	1	0	3
1974/75	13(4)	1	0	3
1975/76	4(3)	1	0	3
1976/77	30	6	0	18
1977/78	32(1)	7	0	21
1978/79	33(1)	10	0	30
1979/80	31(1)	6	0	18
1980/81	24	2	0	6
1981/82	26(3)	0	0	0
1982/83	4	0	0	0
1983/84	19(4)	0	0	0
TOTAL	239(25)	34	0	102

Debut: v. Leigh (A), 16 January 1972
Finals: Rugby League Cup 1979/80 (lost),
1981/82 (won replay); Premiership Trophy
1980/81 (lost), 1981/82 (lost); BBC Floodlit
Trophy 1979/80 (won)

For sheer guts and determination, Keith Tindall stands out as a true hero of Hull FC. Written off early in his career as little more than a reserve-team regular, he battled through shattering injuries and severe illness to become an international prop.

His fighting spirit reached extraordinary heights early in 1979 when he was rushed to hospital with viral meningitis only a few days after being selected to make his England debut. Anybody seeing him lying in an oxygen tent would have assumed that his playing days were over, yet less than three weeks later, and only twelve days after being discharged from hospital, he was back in the Hull front row – and scored both tries in an 8-8 Rugby League Challenge Cup third round draw at Bradford Northern. He also played in the replay three days later. The remarkable recovery was complete the following month when he made his debut for England.

Less than a year later, he got another England call-up, only to have to withdraw yet again. This time it was because of three small broken bones at the base of his back. Once more Tindall defied all logic to be back in action within two weeks and join Hull's Challenge Cup run to Wembley.

The son of Jack Tindall, who played for Hull in the 1940s, Keith was used to battling against the odds. After being signed from local amateur rugby, he spent five years with the reserves and made little impact when he got the occasional first-team call. 'Too light and not rough enough' was a popular view.

It all changed in October 1976 when he received a late call to play at Keighley in a Floodlit Trophy tie. Tindall produced a storming display that boosted his confidence and gave his critics a rethink. From then on he went from strength to strength and became a first-team regular for the next six seasons.

Although he was always to the fore and shirked nothing in Hull's toughest games, many thought he still lacked aggression. It was probably this that restricted his representative appearances to one for England and three for Yorkshire, but Tindall showed his true grit yet again when he battled back from a broken leg to have one last season with Hull in 1983/84.

David Topliss
Stand-off, 1981-85

Season	Apps	Tries	Goals	Pts
1981/82	27(2)	13	2(2)	41
1982/83	37	24	0	72
1983/84	29(1)	15	0	60
1984/85	26(4)	4	0	16
TOTAL	120(7)	56	2(2)	189

Debut: v. Leeds (H), 16 August 1981
Finals: Rugby League Cup 1981/82 (drew, then won replay, 2 tries), 1982/83 (lost); Premiership Trophy 1981/82 (lost), 1982/83 (lost, 1 try); Yorkshire Cup 1982/83 (won), 1983/84 (won); John Player Trophy 1984/85 (lost)

Having recruited a formidable pack in their ambitious rebuilding plans of the late 1970s and early 1980s, Hull set about providing a top-class back division to capitalise on their power. The priority was a quality stand-off with plenty of experience. Wakefield Trinity's Dave Topliss fitted the bill perfectly and they got him for a bargain £15,000 in May 1981. Although Topliss had been at Wakefield for thirteen seasons and, at thirty-one, was supposedly past his peak, he was to have the best years of his playing career at Hull.

He was made captain and in his inaugural season led them to their first Rugby League Challenge Cup success for sixty-eight years. Topliss gave outstanding performances in both the drawn final at Wembley and the glorious replay victory at Elland Road, Leeds. His two-try replay performance won him the Man of the Match award, but the Lance Todd Trophy had already been awarded to Widnes centre Eddie Cunningham after the Wembley game.

In his match-winning replay display, Topliss produced all the skills that had made him one of the top half-backs of the era. He was the key fig-

ure in a devastating four-minute first-half spell that shattered Widnes. Two superbly executed moves from scrums resulted in Topliss sending over Gary Kemble for the first try and finishing off the second himself. Widnes hit back to be only a point behind midway through the second half when Topliss struck again, darting through for a try that put Hull back in full command.

There was bitter disappointment the following season when Featherstone Rovers beat them at Wembley and they lost to Widnes in the Premiership final after Topliss had opened the try scoring. But Topliss had already led them to the Championship and victory in the Yorkshire Cup final. He had played a huge part in their successes, playing in 37 matches and scoring 24 tries. One of the tries was Hull's only touchdown in an epic encounter with Australia, who were given their toughest match of the 1982 tour before winning 13-7. The try was also one of only seven conceded by the Kangaroos on that trip.

Despite Topliss's outstanding form, it still came as a surprise when he was called up for the third Test – and appointed Great Britain's captain. That Topliss never gave a thought to being selected became obvious when it was learned that he was on holiday in Majorca. It was one of four Test appearances he made for Britain, but the only time as a Hull player. Topliss's first-team place came under threat in 1983/84 when the club signed New Zealand international stand-off Fred Ah Kuoi, but when the Kiwi was injured

David Topliss on the attack against Leeds in a 1984/85 John Player Special Trophy semi-final.

Topliss partnered Peter Sterling during the Australian Test scrum-half's first brief spell with Hull. After Sterling returned home, Topliss retained the stand-off spot with Ah Kuoi moving to scrum-half. The rivalry continued throughout the next season, and when Ah Kuoi was preferred for the Cup final at Wembley Topliss knew it was time to move on. His last game for Hull had been a week earlier when he signed off with a try in a 46-12 Premiership first round defeat at Wigan.

Although Topliss was only at Hull for four seasons, his impact had been tremendous – both as a captain and as an individual. His partnership with loose forward Norton was at the heart of many of their greatest victories. Topliss was a rarity among stand-offs in the 1970s and 1980s in that he was both a creator and finisher. There may have been a few who were a little better at either, but none who had both skills in such abundance.

Even after he joined Oldham in May 1985, well into the veteran stage, he had two good seasons before returning to Wakefield as their player-coach in May 1987. He took them to promotion in his first season and finished his playing career in their last match. Topliss remained as coach until April 1994 when he decided to take a break from the game he had served so well.

In addition to his successes at Hull, he had won the Lance Todd Trophy with Wakefield despite their defeat by Widnes in the 1979 final. In the same year he was flown out as a replacement on Great Britain's tour of Australia and New Zealand. Topliss had already made a big impression in Australia during spells with Penrith and Balmain. After a while out of the game, Topliss returned to Hull in an advisory capacity, but it did not work out and he did not stay long. His experience remained in demand, however, and he was appointed manager of Yorkshire for their first Origin match against Lancashire in 2001.

Carl Turner
Centre, 1949-59

Season	Apps	Tries	Goals	Pts
1948/49	7	1	0	3
1949/50	28	4	5	22
1950/51	15	0	2	4
1951/52	9	4	0	12
1952/53	40	8	1	26
1953/54	36	10	8	46
1954/55	38	15	0	45
1955/56	28	2	1	8
1956/57	46	19	0	57
1957/58	32	8	0	24
1958/59	7	0	0	0
TOTAL	286	71	17	247

Debut: v. Wakefield T. (A), 26 March 1949
Finals: Championship 1955/56 (won), 1956/57
(lost, 1 try); Yorkshire Cup 1953/54 (lost),
1954/55 (lost), 1955/56 (drew, then lost replay)

Wales has produced many top-class rugby league players. Some arrived in a blaze of publicity and hundreds more came unheralded. One of the latter was Carl Turner, who warranted hardly a line in the national press when he left Kenfig Hill Rugby Union club for Hull in 1949, but he stayed for ten years and gave the club great service as a centre or stand-off.

Turner had been captain of Kenfig and also played for Gloucester, Maesteg and Aberavon. He left Wales as a promising young centre, but it was four years before he really settled into rugby league and began to make an impact. His first match for Hull was as centre to the brilliant Bruce Ryan, and they played together several times before the Australian winger left for Leeds.

It was in the 1950s, when Hull's mighty pack began to dominate the opposition, that Turner started to make his mark as an exciting attacking player. His sometimes erratic play would occasionally turn the Hull crowd against him, but none would question his commitment.

Although Turner gained no international honours in either code, he often subdued more illustrious opponents with his deadly tackling. His versatility also became more important, and after playing centre in all three successive Yorkshire Cup finals plus a replay, he was stand-off for the 1956 Championship final. It was thought to be a big blow when injury ruled free-scoring stand-off Rowley Moat out of the play-off matches, but Turner, who was on the transfer list at £500, stepped in to play a big role in the shock semi-final win at Warrington and the defeat of Halifax in the final.

He was back in the centre a year later when Hull defended their title against Oldham in the final. There was no winners' medal this time, despite Hull taking an early lead when Turner finished off a brilliant all-out attack with a try between the posts. It had been an impressive season for him, however, as he had shown outstanding consistency playing in all but one of Hull's 47 cup and League matches.

Turner was a regular for most of the next season, but was dropped late on and missed the Championship final defeat of Workington Town. He played a few more matches in 1958/59 before transferring to Doncaster.

Tevita Vaikona
Centre, 1994-97

Season	Apps	Tries	Goals	Pts
1994/95	27	8	0	32
1995/96	16	15	0	60
1996	20	16	0	64
1997	32	40	0	160
TOTAL	95	79	0	316

Debut: v. Bradford N. (H), 2 October 1994
Finals: Divisional Premiership 1997 (lost)

Hull fans reacted with fury when Tevita Vaikona was transferred to Bradford Bulls in a £100,000 deal in March 1998. Their anger was understandable. The young Tongan had become a great favourite at The Boulevard and had just completed a season in which his 40 tries were the most by a Hull player since Jack Harrison scored a record 52 touchdowns 82 years earlier. Vaikona had also been voted the Division One Player of the Year by his fellow professionals, after playing a major role in Hull gaining promotion to Super League, and, at only twenty-three, his best years were ahead of him.

Even allowing for the weakness of some of the opposition and four matches on the wing, Vaikona's 40 tries in 32 matches was an exceptional strike rate for a centre. It included six hat-tricks and there was a period when he seemed unstoppable, as he charged in for 16 tries in seven matches. Yet only a few years before he joined Hull, the Tongan knew very little about the city or rugby league. Brought up on a little island of fewer than 600 people, he first dabbled in the game when he went to Christchurch University in New Zealand to study accountancy.

Ironically, it was Mark Broadhurst a former Hull Kingston Rovers forward and veteran of many a derby battle against Hull, who got him to take rugby league seriously after being impressed by his pace and power. With greater dedication he was soon representing Canterbury Under-19s and then the Junior Kiwis on their 1993 tour of Britain.

A successful tour resulted in a few offers from Australia before Hull persuaded the young student to join them. Although Hull were beaten by Bradford Northern on his debut, the *Yorkshire Post* correspondent was prompted to write: 'There were signs of better times ahead for Hull in the performance of Tevita Vaikona. The 6ft 2in Tongan centre showed flashes of real class. He moves quickly into his stride and is remarkably light on his feet for such a big man.'

It took him a little time to settle and he was moved out to the wing before reclaiming his centre spot the following season. Tonga called him up for a couple of games in the 1995 World Cup and it was not long before Super League clubs started to take notice. Hull also had a link-up with local rugby union club Hull Ionians and he was loaned out to them for a few matches in 1997, but the real blow for Hull fans came a few months later when he left rather reluctantly for Bradford, where all of his potential was fulfilled, although mostly on the wing. His last match for Hull had been in the disappointing 18-0 Premiership Division final defeat by Huddersfield.

George Watt

Hooker, 1947-51

Season	Apps	Tries	Goals	Pts
1947/48	29	4	0	12
1948/49	37	2	1	8
1949/50	22	3	0	9
1950/51	2	0	0	0
TOTAL	90	9	1	29

Debut: v. Huddersfield (H), 25 October 1947 (1 try)

The early post-war years saw several top-class Australian players join British clubs. Among them were a number of Test players, including George Watt, who signed for Hull in 1947. This was a terrific coup by the club, for Watt was the top hooker in Australia, having played in all three Test matches against the Great Britain tourists the year before. He was also New South Wales' hooker and earned Grand Final winners' medals with Balmain and Eastern Suburbs.

Hooking was in his blood, for he came from a family of No.9s well known in Australia. His father had played for Balmain and an uncle, Horrie Watt, appeared in three Test matches for Australia against Great Britain in 1924.

Craggy-faced, with a mass of black, wavy hair, George Watt was twenty-nine when he arrived at Hull and looked the part as 'the best conditioned man playing rugby league in Australia'. That is how he was described shortly after signing for Hull and the report also said he had a reputation as one of the most prolific try-scoring hookers in Australian rugby league. He immediately backed up the tryscoring claim on his debut

for Hull by scoring one of their two tries in an 8-0 home defeat of Huddersfield in October 1947. However, it was to be only one of nine he would score in three full seasons with Hull.

There was no doubting his all-round ability, however, and in the days when there were up to 50 scrums in a match, he remained among the game's top strikers for possession. Confirmation that he would have been in the 1948 Kangaroos' squad had he not joined Hull came when he out-hooked his opposite number two to one in the tourists' match against the Airlie Birds. At 5ft 9in and 12st 7lb, he packed plenty of power into his compact build and was at his best when the going was toughest. His leadership qualities were also recognised when Hull appointed him captain.

Watt was one of five Australians Hull signed in the later 1940s – the others being Bruce Ryan, Duncan Jackson, Keith Gittoes and Johnny Payne – but they played together only once before gradually drifting away. Watt stayed for just over three seasons before the former Australian Test star was replaced by a young Welsh hooker who was to achieve even greater international acclaim with Great Britain – Tommy Harris.

Watt's last match for Hull was on 26 March 1951 at Halifax, when a young Mick Scott and Johnny Whiteley were in the pack and Jim Drake made his debut at full-back. A new era was beginning at The Boulevard and the now veteran Australian moved on for a brief spell at Rochdale Hornets before retiring.

Ivor Watts
Winger, 1945-59

Season	Apps	Tries	Goals	Pts
1945/46	27	13	4	47
1946/47	30	10	0	30
1947/48	13	2	0	6
1948/49	3	0	0	0
1949/50	27	4	0	12
1950/51	24	6	0	18
1951/52	40	19	1	59
1952/53	33	19	0	57
1953/54	41	32	0	96
1954/55	35	16	0	48
1955/56	27	16	0	48
1956/57	38	30	0	90
1957/58	30	29	0	87
1958/59	38	15	0	45
1959/60	6	5	0	15
TOTAL	**410**	**216**	**5**	**658**

Debut: v. Batley (H), 27 October 1945 (1 try)
Finals: Rugby League Cup 1958/59 (lost);
Championship 1956/57 (lost), 1957/58 (won);
Yorkshire Cup 1946/47 (lost), 1953/54 (lost),
1955/56 (drew, 1 try, then lost replay)

Hull's second most prolific try scorer with 216, and seventh in their appearances chart, Ivor Watts was a little winger much loved by The Boulevard crowd. He would have scored more tries and added to his 410 appearances had his early years not coincided with Bruce Ryan's time at Hull, but once the brilliant Australian had been transferred to Leeds, Watts began his long occupation of the left-wing berth.

Although Welsh-born, Watts moved to Cumberland when he was seven and, as a youth, had a choice of playing professional soccer or rugby league. He had trials with Workington FC and was also attracting interest from Workington Town Rugby League club. Hull trainer-coach Joe Oliver had also been impressed by the youngster and persuaded him to come for trials. Watts agreed and was signed, scoring a try on his debut.

Within a year he was making the first of his 12 appearances for Cumberland and had become a firm favourite with Hull fans, especially the Threepenny Stand faithful who loved his touch-line-hugging runs. He endeared himself even more when he scored two tries in his first derby game against Hull Kingston Rovers. His tries against Rovers were a forerunner of what was to follow, as he produced some of his best performances in derby matches and twice scampered in for four tries against them. His total of 15 tries against Rovers remains a derby record.

Twelve years after his debut, Watts was still going strong and picked up a Championship winning medal when Hull beat his old home town club, Workington Town, in the 1958 final. He was at Wembley the following year when he was up against the massive and great Billy Boston, who scored two tries in Wigan's victory. Watts' long career was drawing to an end and he played his last game in September 1959, after scoring a career-best five tries in his penultimate match, but Watts stayed on at The Boulevard in a coaching role and, in 1970, took over as the first-team coach after Johnny Whiteley left for Rovers. He was not a success, however, and departed after three depressing years for the club.

Johnny Whiteley
Loose forward, 1950-65

Season	Apps	Tries	Goals	Pts
1950/51	14	2	0	6
1951/52	30	13	0	39
1952/53	31	7	2	25
1953/54	39	11	0	33
1954/55	33	10	0	30
1955/56	41	22	0	66
1956/57	47	18	0	54
1957/58	37	18	0	54
1958/59	26	15	0	45
1959/60	31	16	0	48
1960/61	34	14	0	42
1961/62	25	8	0	24
1962/63	0	0	0	0
1963/64	3	0	0	0
1964/65	26	2	0	6
TOTAL	417	156	2	472

Debut: v. York (A), 23 December 1950
Finals: Rugby League Cup 1958/59 (lost),
1959/60 (lost); Championship 1955/56 (won),
1956/57 (lost), 1957/58 (won, 1 try); Yorkshire
Cup 1953/54 (lost), 1954/55 (lost), 1955/56
(drew, then lost replay), 1959/60 (lost, 1 try)

If you were to ask who the greatest and the most popular Hull-born players of all-time are, the answer to both must be Johnny Whiteley. Few players anywhere achieved the popularity that Johnny Whiteley did at Hull. From the time he made his debut in 1950 through to his last match fifteen years later, Whiteley was acclaimed as much for his gentlemanly conduct as his brilliant loose-forward play. He was never sent off and not for nothing was he called 'Gentleman John' in an era when other top forwards were known as 'Wild Bull' and 'Rocky'.

Arguments still rage as to who was the best in a golden age of loose forwards, but there can be little doubt Whiteley was the classiest. To see Whiteley break away, toes pointed forward in a long, gazelle-like stride, was one of the joys of a game often dominated by fierce trench warfare forward play. Yet he was also a tremendous tackler, with none better at breaking quickly from a scrum to smother the opposition's half back.

Whiteley played in all 10 finals, including a replay, during his fifteen years as a Hull player and was the captain in half of them. He led them to victory against Workington Town in the 1958 Championship when he scored a try, but suffered disappointments with defeats at Wembley in the next two seasons.

Brought up in the Hessle Road area of Hull's then thriving fishing industry, Whiteley never played rugby league at school but enjoyed countless games of it in the street and was a regular visitor to The Boulevard. When he left school, he played soccer for Fish Trades until he joined Hull Boys Club and began playing organised rugby league for the first time. National Service then intervened and he excelled at swimming and rugby union in the Army.

Not long after being demobbed, he played two trial matches for Hull A and signed for £100. He was immediately promoted to the first team and it soon became apparent that he was a player of exceptional ability. A superbly built athlete, his long legs were accentuated in the briefest of shorts when baggies were still the trend. The youngster was a founder member of the great Hull pack that was to dominate the 1950s, his classic

Johnny Whiteley introduces the Duke of Edinburgh to Mike Smith and Tommy Sutton before the 1960 Rugby League Challenge Cup final against Wakefield Trinity at Wembley.

style complementing the more aggressive approach of the other forwards.

A fitness fanatic, Whiteley turned his work, as a fish dock worker and later brewery man, into body-building exercises as he humped the crates around. It all paid off, as representative honours began to flow, completing his career with 15 Test and World Cup appearances for Great Britain, one for England and 12 for Yorkshire. He also captained Great Britain and in 1958 was a member of the outstanding tour squad that retained the Ashes in Australia.

Whiteley was appointed Hull's captain in 1956 and, following the departure of Roy Francis to Leeds, took over as player-coach in October 1963. An ankle injury had caused him to miss the whole of the previous season and limited him to only three matches in 1963/64.

He continued playing for a little longer until his last appearance, at Warrington on 6 February 1965. As coach, he took Hull to two Yorkshire Cup finals, losing to Hull Kingston Rovers in 1967 and beating Featherstone Rovers two years later to bring the Cup back for the first time in forty-six years. His greatest coaching achievement came in 1970 when he was in charge of the most successful ever Great Britain tour squad and the last to win the Ashes. However, there was a shock for Hull when he returned, as he left to become coach of local rivals Hull Kingston Rovers in August 1970.

Things did not work out at Rovers, however, and he was sacked in February 1972, despite having won the Yorkshire Cup a few months earlier. Although that was the end of Whiteley's club connections, he continued as Yorkshire's coach for twelve years and was recalled to take charge of Great Britain for two years from 1980.

Stan Whitty
Stand-off, 1919-31

Season	Apps	Tries	Goals	Pts
1919/20	3	0	0	0
1920/21	0	0	0	0
1921/22	0	0	0	0
1922/23	24	6	0	18
1923/24	36	6	0	18
1924/25	22	11	0	33
1925/26	42	17	0	51
1926/27	43	10	0	30
1927/28	48	7	0	21
1928/29	29	9	0	27
1929/30	14	1	0	3
1930/31	10	0	0	0
TOTAL	271	67	0	201

Debut: v. York (A), 27 December 1919
Finals: Rugby League Cup 1922/23 (lost);
Yorkshire Cup 1923/24 (won), 1927/28 (lost)

One of the greatest half-back partnerships formed at Hull was that of Stan Whitty and Eddie Caswell in the 1920s. Although they made their debuts within a couple of months of each other in 1919, they did not come together as a partnership until two years later. Then you rarely mentioned one without the other, as they formed Hull's half-back pair in over 150 matches. They worked in perfect harmony behind a powerful pack, particularly when they played a key role in Hull's 1923 Yorkshire Cup final defeat of Huddersfield.

However, they were also outstanding players in their own right. Unlike Caswell, a Welshman, Whitty was a local product who joined them as a teenager shortly after the First World War. His debut, at centre, in 1919 was cut short when the match at York was abandoned because of appalling ground conditions, and it was another three years before he became a first-team regular.

Then Hull soon began to benefit from his all-round skills and, in his first full season, he played a major role in the Airlie Birds reaching the Rugby League Challenge Cup final. Ironically,

after missing the first three rounds, it was in the centre that he made his first big impact, as he scored two of Hull's three tries in the 13-9 semi-final defeat of Wigan. However, it all went wrong in the final as Hull were beaten 28-3 by Leeds with Whitty again in the centre.

He was back at stand-off alongside Caswell the following season, and the pair worked their magic to bring the Yorkshire Cup to The Boulevard for the first time, after beating Huddersfield 10-4 in the final. The duo was still together four years later when Hull reached the county final again, only to lose 8-2 to Dewsbury.

Although Whitty and Caswell were undoubtedly one of the best club half-back pairs of their era, neither played in a Test match for Great Britain, but Whitty did go on the 1924 Lions tour of Australia and New Zealand, playing in 14 matches and scoring five tries. Although Whitty was by no means a certainty to be chosen for the tour, he clinched his selection with outstanding performances in two trial matches.

Despite continuing to shine for Hull, there were no further international calls after the tour and he never played for England, but Yorkshire finally acknowledged his talents and he made five appearances for the county.